Creating
Primary Classroom

Creating a Learner-centred Primary Classroom is an essential resource to improve teaching practice, examining the key elements that contribute to a learner-centred classroom and offering strategies to encourage children to take a shared role in their learning.

Including case studies describing teachers' methods for linking theory to practice, this user-friendly, photocopiable resource demonstrates how to:

- Construct a learning community
- Encourage collaborative learning
- Share strategies for engaging individual learners
- Provide a scaffold for strategic thinking in the classroom
- Link assessment procedures to learning
- Showcase the practice and outcomes of purposeful curriculum planning.

Any teacher who wants to tailor their teaching practice to meet the needs of individual learners will find this an invaluable resource.

Kath Murdoch is an experienced teacher who lectured at the University of Melbourne for over a decade.

Jeni Wilson is an associate of the Faculty of Education at the University of Melbourne.

Creating a Learner-centred Primary Classroom

Learner-centred strategic teaching

Kath Murdoch and Jeni Wilson

Routledge
Taylor & Francis Group

LONDON AND NEW YORK

First published 2004 as *Learning Links*, by Curriculum Corporation
PO Box 177
Carlton South
Victoria 3053
Australia

This edition published 2008 by Routledge
2 Park Square, Milton Park, Abingdon, Oxon OX14 4RN

Simultaneously published in the USA and Canada
by Routledge
270 Madison Ave, New York, NY 10016

Routledge is an imprint of the Taylor & Francis Group, an informa business

Typeset in Garamond and Helvetica by
RefineCatch Limited, Bungay, Suffolk
Printed and bound in Great Britain by
Antony Rowe Ltd, Chippenham, Wiltshire

British Library Cataloguing in Publication Data
A catalogue record for this book is available from the British Library

Library of Congress Cataloging in Publication Data
A catalog record for this book has been requested

Photography by Mark Coulson
Artwork by Aja Bongiorno

ISBN10: 0–415–45432–8 (pbk)
ISBN10: 0–203–93112–2 (ebk)

ISBN13: 978–0–415–45432–2 (pbk)
ISBN13: 978–0–203–93112–7 (ebk)

To Ethan and Madison who teach me so many important things. (JW)

To Gretta and Holly who keep me linked to learning about life every day.
Thank you. (KM)

Contents

Acknowledgements

We have been developing the ideas presented in this book for several years. During that time, we have worked with hundreds of teachers and their students, who have contributed in many ways to our understanding of student-centred teaching and learning. We thank all those with whom we have worked, together with our students and colleagues at the University of Melbourne.

Several teachers provided specific ideas from their classroom, advice or feedback on the manuscript. They are Gill Aulich, Carol Braybrook, Nadine Crane, Sarah Cuthbertson, Nerida Eastoe, Robyn English, Lidia Foskett, Vanessa Forster, Kath Gillick Maher, Dean Goodridge, Fiona Graham, Roger Harlow, Colleen Holloway, Pam Hoyne, Rebecca Hoyne, Sue Lalor-Capewell, David Lee, Suzanne Lowe, Natalie Miller, Joy Moodley, Jo Parry, Bronwyn Prismall, Karen Richardson, Wendy Richmond, Robert Roe, Jo Schwartz, Andrew Starrick, Teresa Stone, Rebecca Walsh and all staff at Hawthorn West Primary School.

Introduction

What's it all about?

This is a book about powerful classroom practice. It is dedicated to supporting teachers in the work they do with their students each day as they go about the task of facilitating learning. Research from around the world continues to conclude that the quality of the teacher is the most significant factor influencing students' learning (Darling-Hammond, 2000). What we do as teachers, and how we do it, makes a difference.

Expectations of what we do and how we do it have changed dramatically over the past few decades. Teaching in current times demands that we focus our decision making around the individual needs of our students. Our classrooms must be places that genuinely offer students a voice – a shared role in their learning journey. There is no doubt that constructing such environments is complex and highly demanding. We must be well versed in pedagogy, learning theories, curriculum planning and design, time management and organisation, quality assessment and team skills. On the one hand, teaching has never been so professionally satisfying and exhilarating; on the other, teachers can feel as if they are drowning in a sea of rapid reform without the tools to manage the changes.

In this book, we examine some of the key elements that contribute to a truly learner-centred classroom. These elements, or links, do not exist in isolation, but are continuous and connected, linking powerful learning and teaching experiences. The elements we explore in each chapter apply to *all* teachers, regardless of the age level or subject areas for which they are responsible. These elements make up our shared, core business as teachers.

It has been our great privilege to work with many teachers who have been exploring ways to shift and shape their practice in response to the challenges of new times. We have been invited to work with teams of teachers in their schools and classrooms for extended periods of time, allowing us to share in very authentic journeys of professional discovery. The impetus for *Creating a Learner-centred Primary Classroom* arose from this work. We firmly believe that classroom practice, and the beliefs that guide it, must be at the very heart of professional learning and, ultimately, of reform.

Learning to learn

Our collective goal as teachers is to help students grow into inquiring and resourceful individuals who can demonstrate what they know and, importantly, what to do when they don't know! In a world of rapidly escalating and changing knowledge, our students must become proficient at selecting, critiquing and applying their learning across a wide range of contexts. It is well accepted that the students we currently teach are much less likely to enter one career for the whole of their working lives. Their experience of work will be unlike any generation before them and is likely to involve several pathways. They will need to be adaptable, flexible, resilient individuals with a capacity to learn and re-learn, and the ability to communicate ideas in multi-modal ways.

Success in learning increasingly depends on generic skills and qualities that can be transferred across time and place. These qualities and skills are not discipline specific and can be considered the province of all teachers working with any age group. Various policy documents across the world have set out to describe what these skills and qualities are. While there are differences in the emphasis given, there is general agreement about many of the core skills and qualities. These are detailed in the figure below.

Effective lifelong learners are:
flexible and adaptable,
creative, resilient, optimistic,
systematic, organised,
good communicators
(multi-modal),
technologically literate,
intelligent in many ways,
open minded, risk takers,
empathetic, reflective,
metacognitive,
self-aware.

Effective lifelong learners think:
ethically, critically, laterally,
logically, analytically,
creatively, reflectively
about their thinking,
about their learning,
about themselves, others
and the physical world.

Effective lifelong learners can:
problem solve, question, cooperate,
make decisions, consider possibilities and
consequences, identify and use a range of
resources, articulate what they know and need
to know, research (locate, gather, critique) and
communicate in a range of ways.

Core attributes of effective lifelong learners

The quest for deeper understanding

Much of the criticism of traditional approaches to curriculum, teaching and learning relates to the low-level thinking they often require of students. Isolated and fragmented, teacher-centred approaches can require a 'regurgitation of facts' which are quickly forgotten and rarely transferred or applied to anything else. It has also been argued that in our efforts to create more caring and supportive classrooms, we have inadvertently 'dumbed down' the curriculum for our students. Classrooms can be both intellectually challenging *and* enjoyable. In fact, by working towards deep understanding and involving students in high-level thinking about significant ideas, the engagement in and passion for learning is increased.

We cannot teach our students everything there is to know. Our role must be to help them work with knowledge in all its complexity; to aim for depth over breadth and to help students develop a conceptual map to navigate their way around a complex and ever changing world. Deep understanding over shallow, short-term retention of facts requires strategic and mindful teaching. Teaching for understanding requires us to be well versed in the art of questioning – to lead students to pose problems, think creatively, consider possible solutions, investigate in a range of ways, analyse data and communicate findings. Teaching for understanding also requires a differentiated approach to working with students, and the ability to assess the needs of individuals in order to plan ways to improve their learning outcomes. Strategic teaching is creative. It strikes a thoughtful balance between the planned and the spontaneous. Above all, strategic teaching depends on authentic and caring relationships with individual students.

What students want

The emergence of interest in upper primary and lower secondary schooling recognises the lack of engagement many young people experience in traditional classrooms. And young people are more likely now than ever before to communicate their feelings to us. Both the anecdotal evidence of many teachers, as well as recent student feedback, conclude that students want relevant, hands-on, authentic learning experiences. As we nurture a generation of young people who are more in tune with themselves as learners, they will come to expect – indeed, to demand – more responsibility for, involvement in and control over the construction of their learning journey. We believe this is their right and it is our responsibility to assist them in developing the skills and knowledge necessary to effectively negotiate learning opportunities.

The science of learning

Research over the past two decades has provided us with a wealth of information about how students learn. In the past, much of our concern as teachers centred around *what* we taught and, often to a lesser degree, *how* we taught it. Increasingly, we must turn our attention to *whom* we teach – to the needs and characteristics of the individual students in our care. As a profession we now have an extensive body of information about learning. We know, for example, that students can learn in profoundly different ways. We know of the importance of connected relevant experiences, of the need to establish prior knowledge before moving students on from their current positions. We know how important reflection and metacognition are to strengthening learning, and the powerful role of sustained dialogue in helping students clarify and communicate their understandings. The world of science has contributed much to our current understandings. We understand more about the way the brain works and about the differences that exist between the learning styles and preferences of individual students. We are in the best position yet to utilise this information to improve our students' learning.

Teachers as learners

If we are to maintain a focus on our core business – that of supporting the learning of students in our care – we need to take time to nurture our *own* learning journey as professionals. No book, programme, curriculum document or education 'guru' can do this for us. Ultimately, the quality of our learning journey depends on the extent to which we bring a reflective and open attitude to all we do – a preparedness to question, take risks, try out new ideas and listen to our students. We hope that teachers will find this book a helpful addition to their continued professional growth.

Using *Creating a Learner-centred Primary Classroom*

High-quality teaching is underpinned by clearly understood, well-informed beliefs about the learning process. *Creating a Learner-centred Primary Classroom* is intended to explicate the principles of student-centred learning and provide practical guidelines and strategies to improve teaching practice. The ideas within the book encourage systematic application of beliefs rather than haphazard implementation of strategies. It is organised in a way that shows the important link between beliefs and practice; between what we do and why we do it. The activities suggested are just a few of those that support the beliefs. Once you are clear about the foundational principles behind each set of activities, we encourage you to explore other similar ideas and make the links between the ideas in each chapter and your own.

Creating a Learner-centred Primary Classroom is also organised in a way that encourages exploration by teams of teachers or a whole staff. Individual chapters can be used as a springboard for collaborative reflection and inquiry to stimulate discussion, help design professional learning projects or help a school create its own teaching and learning policy/statement. Each chapter of the book explores one of the elements identified in the figure on page 2, as well as identifying some links between this element and others. Importantly, the information in each chapter is designed to provide a broad overview – a springboard for thinking about and working with the element described. Interested teachers can then use the bibliography (page 113) to continue more detailed investigations.

Each chapter is organised as follows:

- *Teaching and learning principles:* a set of major principles related to the focus area.
- *Introductory statement:* a brief theoretical overview and rationale.
- *Making it happen:* a set of broad guidelines to help link theory to practice at whole school and classroom level.
- *Something to try:* several practical strategies for classroom application, each including purposes, step-by-step instructions and ideas for extension and adaptation (see page 6 for a full list of strategies).
- *Snapshots:* case studies describing one school's or classroom teacher's way of linking theory to practice.

Strategies described in this book

1 If you build it they will learn
Constructing a learning community

Teaching and learning principles

- The relationships teachers build with their students profoundly impact on their learning.
- Each learner needs to feel valued for who they are.
- A learning community is more effective when open mindedness and risk taking are encouraged.
- Shared laughter can build classroom team spirit.
- Learners will take risks and embrace challenges in an environment that feels safe, supportive and secure.
- Learners benefit from playing an active role in classroom decision making.
- Clear goals, processes, expectations, rules, routines and a discipline plan enable students to take more responsibility for learning.
- Understanding the learning process and personal learning attributes enhances learning.

Introductory statement

Building an effective learning community is fundamental to each of the aspects of strategy teaching explored in this book. The idea of a 'learning community' can be used to describe a school or other organisations. In this chapter, we explore the notion in relation to the classroom.

We believe that taking the time and effort to build an effective learning community is not only worth it, but crucial for constructive learning. By nurturing a community of learners in our classrooms, we help position students to collaborate, think, inquire and act more effectively. This involves three key elements:

- creating a positive team spirit
- helping students learn about learning
- skill development (see also Chapter 2).

Feeling valued as a team member can encourage risk taking and motivate learners to think, perform and make responsible learning decisions. Without a healthy classroom team spirit, students can feel isolated, lack motivation and be inhibited or destructive in their relationships and behaviour. When students have a positive self-concept, trust and communicate well with their peers and teachers, and have fun together, they are more likely to be receptive to learning and self-appraisal (the latter is discussed in Chapter 6).

While the importance of team building is increasingly being recognised, it is sometimes considered 'done' in the first week. Teachers often spend time at the beginning of the year getting to know students personally, learning names and negotiating rules, but this team building needs to be frequently revisited throughout the year. We believe that an effective classroom community requires regular 'servicing'. The frequency of this depends on classroom personalities and dynamics.

The relationships we have with our students – both collectively and individually – are at the heart of our teaching. This chapter offers some ideas for establishing, reviewing and maintaining constructive classroom relationships where all students feel a respected and important part of the team. It also outlines guidelines and strategies for focussing on learning. This relies on establishing core rules, routines and a discipline plan.

Making it happen: guidelines for constructing a learning community

Establishing core rules, routines and a discipline plan

When students understand and are part of establishing the class (and individual) goals, rules and discipline plan, they feel greater ownership and take more responsibility for learning. This important part of the beginning-of-the-year routine helps to raise the issues of common rights and responsibilities, to value the community of learners and to reinforce the importance of democratic processes. This is a time to reassure students that it is safe to learn and that you expect everyone to treat others with respect.

Once reasonable and agreed rules and routines are established these need to be consistently and positively reinforced. Class time is learning time and the class rules should enforce this. A plan for corrective discipline should be established in advance and be seen to be fair and respectful to all. Rogers (1995) argues that when teachers approach the issue of discipline with respect for students' dignity and humanity, they will respond positively. Otherwise, we risk losing the cooperation and goodwill of the class. The smooth execution of this is underpinned by teachers and their ability to maintain respectful, calm and constructive relationships with each individual despite any discipline hiccups. (See Chapter 2 for further ideas involving students in developing protocols and organisation for shared decision making.)

Getting to know everybody

When teachers can truly understand the uniqueness of each student and their learning preferences, they are in a better position to develop a curriculum that is responsive to their needs and contributes positively to their learning outcomes. Parents often view great teachers as those who have 'suited their child'. It is our belief that children should not be moulded to suit a teacher. Instead, teachers should cater for and accommodate the needs of each child, bring out their highly individualised talents and develop a love of learning. Understanding students means taking the time to find out about them, their interests, home lives, skills and their preferred learning styles.

The strategies in this chapter have been designed to help teachers get to know students – their goals, self-beliefs and preferred learning conditions. Parents are also a great source of information about children. Many teachers set up a brief information night at the beginning of the year to find out about their students from parents. Some schools ask parents to write to them about their children. This requires little work on behalf of the teacher but reveals much useful information.

Dear Ms Rae,

Tom is a very active boy who likes to do things his own way. He can be very creative and he enjoys a challenge. He is persistent and keeps trying. He can also be very stubborn. Sometimes we think Tom is not listening when he's wiggling and fiddling but he is.

He worries about his brother because Jack is sick a lot. Please remember he is younger than most of the other students. We hope you can see the good in him and that you can help him develop confidence.

Hope this helps,

Fiona and Steve

Build trusting relationships

Developing trusting relationships among students and with teachers can promote better communication and minimise behavioural problems. Teachers can help break down the power relationships that exist in some classrooms and inhibit the development of trusting relationships. For example, teachers might tell students why they are lucky to have them as a teacher and then ask students to tell them why the teacher is fortunate to have them in the class.

You're so lucky to have me in your grade Mrs Eastoe because I like maths and I can do big sums. I finish my work fast.

The A Letter to My Teacher worksheet (page 23) provides a written structure to collect information that might be the basis for developing relationships. The following questions could also be used for the same purpose at a class or individual level:

- How do you feel about your learning?
- What are you looking forward to this year/term?
- What do you really want to learn?
- What annoys you at school?
- What worries you about learning?
- What do you want your teacher to know about you?
- What could you do to help others at school?
- What excites you about learning?
- What motivates you to want to learn?
- What are some of your goals for this year?
- What are some of your challenges for this year?
- How do you want the teacher to help you learn?

A 'Worries Postbox' can be placed in the classroom for students to post their concerns. Ensure the concerns are responded to promptly or students will stop using the postbox.

Shared decision making

Where joint decision making is used in the classroom, teacher preparation is important. Teachers must first decide on what's negotiable and what's not. Some aspects of the curriculum that may be considered for negotiation are classroom activities, rules, routines, homework and assessment.

Approaches to negotiation can vary. For example, learning centres, projects or contracts might be used to negotiate classroom activities. Parameters relating to length of time or who is involved must also be considered and made explicit.

Value individuals and develop self-esteem

Frequent and explicit demonstrations that we value each other's ideas and contributions help to build self-esteem. Pats on the back (literal and metaphoric) at the end of the day are a nice way to encourage the values we respect at school. For example, the teacher might say, 'I'd like to give Ethan a pat on the back for listening so well today. Who else would like to give someone a pat on the back?' This can be varied in many ways, focusing on recognising individual strengths.

As visitors to classrooms, we are often surprised to find that students do not know everybody else's names. The importance of this should not be underestimated. Not knowing (or using) others' names makes it hard to communicate effectively and work with others. When names are used, a person's contribution is publicly acknowledged. One frequently used classroom method for learning names and the qualities of individuals is to construct a class directory or website (see Chapter 4).

Develop communication skills

Communication skills depend on a healthy team spirit and both are essential for effective cooperative team work. Two important communication skills are active listening and assertive speaking. The former is often considered a problem in classrooms and requires much reinforcement and frequent teacher modelling.

The importance of communication skills must be clearly demonstrated to students. For example, activities that require students to follow directions to achieve a group goal are useful. Simulation and role-play can also highlight difficulties associated with ineffective communication. The Fishbowl strategy (page 28) can be used to demonstrate communication skills.

It is useful to spend time reflecting on and reinforcing important communication skills and preferred ways of working with each other. The table below is an example of a classroom chart that could be created with or for students. This table could be added to by students or teachers.

It makes a difference . . .		
What you:	**If you:**	**How you:**
think	care	share
say	trust	talk
do	thank	act
dream	risk	play
invent	laugh	live
feel	listen	learn
create	question	teach
decide	judge	work
value	smile	communicate
understand	empathise	
	give	
	invite	
	praise	
	plan	

Foster shared laughter and fun

As adults, we know how important it is to have a laugh while learning and/or working. This is also true for students. If our ego is strong enough, having a laugh at ourselves is also worthwhile, but under no circumstances is laughing at others in classrooms appropriate.

Research into students' perceptions of school (particularly in the years spanning upper primary and lower secondary) indicates that many students find school boring, a drudgery and sometimes worse. It can make a big difference to the attitude of individuals and the class when students and teachers enjoy themselves. It is a useful teacher question to ask: Would I like to be a student in my own classroom?

Two concepts that we believe complement shared laughter and enjoyment at school are open-mindedness and risk taking. A classroom climate where these are accepted as the norm is helpful. Risk taking (not physically dangerous) and open-mindedness should be seen as legitimate and useful avenues for learning. They can be validated through regular teacher modelling and reinforcement.

Shared laughter should not be left to the kids! A sense of joy, fun and optimism is also important for staff wellbeing. Whole school special events or foci, such as performances, can promote unity between staff and students.

Learn about learning and thinking

Having high self-confidence and being a good team member are more likely when students have a good understanding of themselves as learners. This is made more possible when students learn that differences are respected and accommodated.

The process of learning how to learn is being increasingly discussed in education circles because of the positive impact this can have on learning. Recognising one's own learning style, strengths and needs can enhance learning significantly, especially when the classroom environment encourages active and student-directed learning.

We believe that students benefit from regular opportunities to focus on and explore the nature of learning. For example, students can be asked to think about what 'learning' means by reflecting on something they have learnt recently at school or at home. A simple practical activity would be to draw up a T-chart to identify the things that helped them learn and the things that hindered their learning. Alternatively, students could interview or survey other students or parents about their learning. A discussion of the similarities and differences reveals much about the different ways that students learn.

The Fishbowl strategy (page 28) can be used to 'watch' each other at work and identify the habits or behaviours of effective learners. Students can also teach each other something and reflect on the skills necessary for effective teaching. Observations can be recorded and documented for review, goal setting and self-assessment purposes.

Some schools have designed lessons or units of work to focus on how the brain works and conditions that enhance and hamper learning. For example, they may ask students to consider the effect of natural light, rest, healthy foods, relaxation, exercise, fresh air, music or drinking water on their learning and then to take some form of action. All of the above examples put the spotlight on the learning process. This sends an important message to students about the value of understanding and reflecting on learning and themselves as learners.

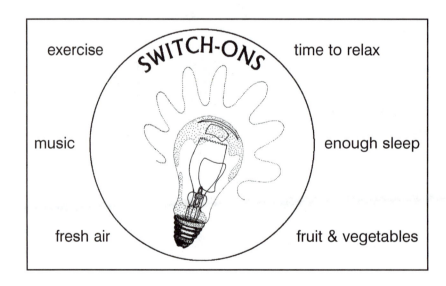

Something to try

Strategy 1

Class Slogans

Creating slogans/mottos or motivational sayings can help build team spirit and provide powerful reminders of agreed protocol or preferred behaviours. This activity could be the start of discussing the importance of positive thinking and optimism.

Directions

1. Ask students to recall some popular slogans or sayings they might know. For example, advertising slogans from television or billboards. Discuss the purpose of slogans: What are they designed to do? Why are they often 'short and sharp'? Note the way that many slogans can accompany visual images or symbols used to capture the essence of a product/company/ approach.

2. Explain to students that they are going to create some posters/symbols to accompany slogans/sayings for display around the room. The following slogans might be used as examples:
   - Reach for the stars
   - Don't dream it, do it
   - Attitude: a small thing with a big impact
   - From little things, big things grow
   - Keep your mind on the big picture
   - Think outside the box
   - It's how you play the game that counts
   - When the going gets tough, the tough get going
   - Today is the first day of the rest of your life

3. Ask students to consider what each slogan/saying means to them. What does it mean in terms of a learning community?

4. Now have students illustrate the slogans/sayings to create posters around the room.

Adaptations/extensions

- Students create their own slogans relating to cooperation, reflection, research, thinking, relationships or other generic aspects of classroom life.
- Generate a list of relevant sayings and have students prioritise them according to those they think are most to least important.
- Create a class motto, symbol, shield or choose a class mascot.

Strategy 2

Personal Goal Setting

The basic belief behind goal setting and other self-assessment strategies is that active student involvement in learning decisions promotes responsibility for and ownership of learning. This is necessary for developing independent learning skills.

Directions

1. Ask students to think about their learning and how they feel they are going. They could discuss this in a small group or as a whole class.

2. Ask students to use the ideas from the discussion to make a plan for their own learning. Specify the context and time span available to them for this. For example, they might have a term learning plan or one that is developed within one learning area such as English.

3. Ask students to record their focus for self-improvement and examples that indicate whether they have achieved their learning goals (see the Going for Goals worksheet on page 22).

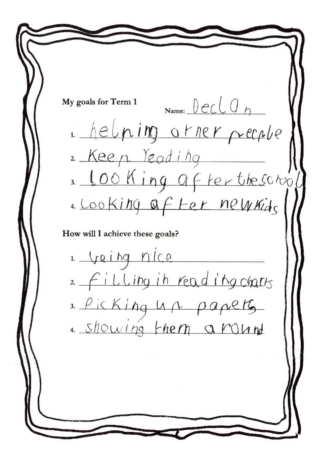

Adaptations/extensions

- Provide some structure for the learning discussion. For example: List the things you are proud of. What do you want to improve? What would be helpful for you to do to improve your learning?
- The Going for Goals worksheet (page 22) specifies particular areas and provides prompts for thinking and planning. Although this is designed for a beginning-of-the-year goal setting, it could also be used for shorter periods of time, such as one term.
- Make time to monitor the goals and reset goals as necessary.

Strategy 3

A Letter to My Teacher

This is a useful beginning-of-the-year strategy to help teachers get to know each student and their learning goals better.

Directions

1. Tell students that you would like to find out more about them personally because this is important for effective learning. Ask: Why is it important for me to know you?
2. Ask students to complete the A Letter to My Teacher worksheet (page 23) or to draft their own letter to tell you about their learning goals, dreams, worries, etc.
3. Make time to meet with students individually or at least in small groups to discuss their hopes for the year. Use this as an opportunity to have them think about what they need to do to achieve these goals and how you can help them with their plan.

Adaptations/extensions

- Model letter writing to students as a class exercise. Alternatively, send individual letters to students as a way of introducing yourself and sharing plans for the year.
- You may find that there are a number of students who have similar hopes (or fears). These could be used as the basis of developing learning plans for or with them. For example, there may be some students who want to learn more about e-learning. A small group of experts could be set up in the class to do this and to then teach others.
- It is important to support the intentions and worries of students, otherwise there is no point in asking about them. If necessary, ongoing interviews with the teacher could be arranged to check how their learning plans are progressing.

Strategy 4

You and Me

To help teachers and students get to know each other, students can interview class members and feed the information back to others. This has the potential to span several sessions. For example, students could be involved in drafting questions, recording interviews and presenting data in a variety of ways.

Directions

1. Ask students what they think would be helpful for you and others in the class to know about individual student learning. A class brainstorm could be used to generate a list of ideas.
2. Students use these ideas to work in small groups to create interview questions. The teacher may wish to check the questions.
3. Students interview at least one class member. It is recommended that teachers choose partners and that students do not interview their friends. Teachers could explain that during the year all students will be expected to work with everyone else in the class. This activity may be the first opportunity for students to get to know and work with class members that they do not usually work with.
4. Students report their findings back to the class.

Adaptations/extensions

- Give example interview questions to students as a starting point.
- Students form small groups where they introduce their interviewee and report their findings orally.
- Students create posters or written reports to share what they have found out about each other. For example, they could start with the heading: Introducing . . .
- Students use technology to record and present their interviews.

Strategy 5

Talk-up Triangle

This activity is primarily designed to develop confidence in speaking assertively and listening actively. It is very useful to discuss common communication difficulties in a non-threatening way. As students speak about their ways of responding to statements they can practise using 'I' statements. This activity can be adapted for other classroom challenges, such as the role of individuals in groups and classroom activities.

Directions

1. Make three signs (words or symbols) to signify three areas: assertive, aggressive and submissive. For example: owl, shark and turtle. Discuss what the terms mean (see the first adaptation and definitions on page 20).

2. Place the words or symbols on the floor (or wall) in the shape of a triangle. The space should be large enough for all students to stand between the symbols/words.

3. Read a scenario (see examples below) to students and ask them to consider how they would respond: assertively, aggressively or submissively. For example: an assertive response might be to say how they feel by starting with 'I'; an aggressive response might be to talk over the top of others and could include put-downs; and a submissive response might be to let everyone else speak without saying how they feel. Remind students that there may be a variety of viewpoints and that alternative views will be heard.

4. Students then physically move to the position that best represents what they would do or say.

5. Students can be interviewed so that they have a chance to explain how they feel and what they would do. This is a chance for them to practise 'I' statements and for others to hear examples of responses that they may not have considered.

Example scenarios:

- You are working in a group and someone keeps dominating the conversation. You have been trying to speak up but no one seems to be listening.

- Your joint project is due but one person hasn't done their share and you want to get a good result.

- You have been waiting for a long time in the canteen queue and it is your turn. Someone pushes in.

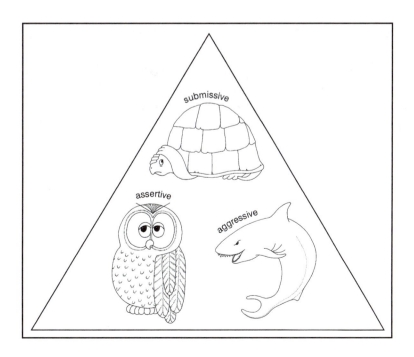

Adaptations/extensions

- Students change their minds and positions after they have heard someone else speak.
- Students generate statements that could be used for the activity.
- Use students' scenarios for role-playing the alternatives.
- Use this activity as a springboard to more activities on conflict resolution.
- Students identify what each position would feel, look and sound like.

Definitions

Assertion is when you clearly state/clarify your own thoughts, feelings and/or needs without impinging on the rights of others. Assertive statements often begin with 'I'. They do not blame others or demand that others give up their needs/rights.

Aggression is when you insist on expressing your own thoughts and feelings regardless of the feelings and rights of others. This may include personal criticism. These statements violate others' rights. Some body language and failing to listen to others people's feelings or needs can be considered another form of aggressive behaviour.

Submission is choosing not to express your own thoughts, feelings and/or needs. You give in to others' demands or wishes without clarifying or expressing your own needs. In this way your own rights are being impinged upon. This is usually because of the fear of aggression or intimidation.

(adapted from Allard, Bretherton and Collins 1992 and Allard and Wilson 1995)

SNAPSHOT

Building a sense of community through a whole school project

Having successfully applied for a grant to fund an artist in residence, the staff at a primary school decided to embark on a whole school cultural and curriculum experience called 'The Spirit of Africa'. An African-born drummer, dancer and storyteller worked intensively in the school for several weeks. During this time, staff and students immersed themselves in finding out about African countries and cultures. They visited African restaurants, learned to dance together, visited a safari park and, most significantly, spent a day co-planning a whole school inquiry-based unit in which students from Reception to Year 6 worked on investigating issues related to African life.

At the end of the term, the school celebrated by hosting a magical night of African drumming, dancing and storytelling in which every student was involved. Students also spent a day visiting each other's classrooms; older and younger children sharing the work they had been doing during the term. In addition to the powerful learning students undertook about culture, identity and diversity, the experience had a significant impact on the 'feeling' across the school. Parents, teachers and students alike commented on the way in which the 'Spirit of Africa' had bonded them in a powerful way.

Teachers had a common focus for their work and students were sharing with each other in new and unexpected ways. 'Undertaking a whole school, shared project, particularly one that is so rich in the arts, has been a great start to the school year,' commented the deputy head. 'I think we need to do something like this at least once a year, to nurture the camaraderie and sense of community we value so highly.'

MY WORKSHEET
Going for Goals

Name: _____

List your one main hope or dream for your learning this year.

_____

List your biggest potential challenge.

_____

What is one risk you would take if you could?

_____

MY GOAL	HOW WILL YOU KNOW IF YOU HAVE ACHIEVED YOUR GOAL?
Behaviour/relationships	
Knowledge	
Skills	
Attitude	
Other	

Personalised Learning in the Primary Classroom © Kath Murdoch and Jeni Wilson, Routledge, 2008

MY WORKSHEET
A Letter to My Teacher

Name: _____

This is your chance to tell your teacher about your learning dreams, goals and worries. Some words are listed on the right of the page to help you describe your feelings. Only use them if they are helpful. Be honest.

Dear

This year I am _____ about my learning.

I would really like to

_____ this year.

My biggest wish for my learning this year is that I

_____

I am wondering

_____

_____

I am hoping that you

_____

_____

My personal learning goals are

_____

From

SUGGESTIONS

excited

keen

concerned

curious

motivated

worried

unsure

prepared

hopeful

interested

challenge

confident

ready

able

happy

hesitant

2 All together now
Helping students to work collaboratively

> **Teaching and learning principles**
> - All students can benefit from collaborative learning.
> - Working collaboratively can result in more efficient use of time.
> - Working collaboratively improves individual thinking and learning.
> - Collaborative learning demonstrates the social power of learning.
> - Effective collaborative learning boosts students' self-esteem and confidence, which are critical to learning.
> - Working collaboratively provides students with the experience of learning from, with and teaching each other, and can help students value diversity and difference.
> - Collaborative skills are fundamental to success in life beyond school.
> - Collaborative work increases the opportunity for enhancing communication skills, participation and responsibility/accountability.

Introductory statement

The ability to work as part of a team is among the most vital things we can teach students. Collaborative skills are cited again and again by employers as highly desirable qualities of their employees – usually prioritised over the specific technical knowledge associated with a job. There is little doubt that the skills associated with effective team work will continue to be vital to successful lifelong learning and active citizenship. Collaborative work provides a context in which students can develop important interpersonal skills for effective social interaction. Working closely with others teaches students to be more sensitive to difference, and to compromise, share and communicate in a range of ways. In short, collaborative learning helps build our students' capacity for healthy relationships with others as well as enhancing their learning outcomes.

Many of the students we teach come from smaller families than those of the past. Today's students generally grow up with less contact with others – preferred activities are often more solitary and confined to the home. Our communities are increasingly fragmented. We share fewer facilities and resources and gather with others less frequently. The classroom may be one of the few places where students are regularly required to share, wait, take turns, compromise and accept criticism. It is vital that we apprentice young people into the 'thinking and the doing' associated with true collaboration from the moment they enter school. Schools themselves – and many contexts beyond schools – require students to participate in discourses consistent with cooperating and working with others. If students are not engaged in such discourses through their home lives, classroom life provides a vital opportunity.

We argue that working collaboratively needs to be a fundamental expectation of all teachers across a school. It should be viewed as part of 'the way we do things around here'. Students need to feel that it is an expectation that they can work collaboratively.

Like other significant generic learning skills, we need to actively and explicitly teach our students how to work collaboratively – right down to details such as the use of body language, eye contact and appropriate language. There are many powerful strategies we can use to help students develop skills and to reflect on the way they work in groups. Working collaboratively in itself offers a rich layer to other strategies – developing skills, understandings and values simultaneously.

Effective classrooms incorporate a wide range of grouping arrangements – pairs, trios, self-selected, teacher-determined, single and mixed gender, mixed ability or needs based. Working collaboratively is important, but it is only one arrangement for student learning. Students also need time to work on their own or as a whole class group. The decisions teachers make about grouping students need to be informed by the purpose of the task itself as well as the classroom dynamics and relationships that exist between students.

Making it happen: guidelines for developing collaboration

Build team spirit

Collaborative learning works better in classrooms where a team spirit and cooperative ethos are part of everything you do. Encourage a 'we' attitude and work to build the sense of community in the classroom as a whole. Groups can develop an identity and team spirit by giving themselves a name, having a mascot or symbol. Many of the ideas outlined in the first chapter work towards the development of team spirit in the classroom.

Teach by example

Use whatever opportunity you can to teach by example. Demonstrate to students how you benefit from collaborative work with others. Team teach when you can, talk about the work you do with your colleagues. Collaborative classroom communities need to be supported by an overarching collaborative school community. Students need to see teachers as team players too!

Consider physical arrangements

Consider the way the furniture and other aspects of the classroom's physical environment are arranged. If tables are grouped in clusters, it is easier for students to work in small groups. The way students are seated can have a real impact on how well the group works. While there should be a place in the room that students can return to as their 'space', establish the understanding that they will not always work there. They need to be comfortable working in various places around the room. Floor space should be available if possible, especially when there are materials that need sorting or spreading out. Flexibility is the key to supporting collaboration through physical spaces. Even very small classrooms can have students working in groups. In fact, grouping tables/desks usually provides more room to move. We have observed that classrooms with a minimum of clutter (and this may mean reducing the amount of materials/work on display) foster a calmer and more focused working atmosphere.

Teach skills explicitly

Many students, particularly those in the early years, need to see collaborative learning in action. They need to learn what cooperation looks, sounds and feels like. Time needs to be spent helping students learn how to assert themselves, disagree respectfully with others, take on various roles within a group, speak clearly and listen actively. Reflection time can be used to focus on collaborative skills and strategies (for example, see the Fishbowl strategy on page 28).

Establish roles and responsibilities

Teach students about the different roles that people can play to maximise the effectiveness of a group. Students should build their capacity to perform each role throughout their schooling and to understand the importance of individual accountability in group work (see the Doing My Bit strategy on page 31). Examples of some of these roles include:

 Encourager (makes a point of ensuring that good ideas are acknowledged and that people are involved)

 'Go-for' (gathers and returns necessary materials)

 Observer (watches and listens to the group, identifying how they are working together, strengths and weaknesses and then reports back to them or the class)

 Organiser (gets the group going and helps keep them on track)

 Problem solver (makes suggestions as to how to sort out a problem if it arises)

 Recorder (records the group's ideas)

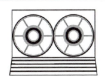 Reporter (reports back to the class, teacher or another group)

 Time keeper (keeps an eye on the clock and lets the group know how long they have to go)

Naturally, while the roles are helpful for many activities there are times when their use is unnecessary or when they need not be explicitly allocated. Sometimes individuals can become so fixated on their roles they lose sight of the tasks at hand.

Include reflection

Students must be given regular opportunities to think about their learning and their behaviour in collaborative contexts. Both formal and informal reflection is a critical component in improving collaborative work in the classroom. Much can be achieved simply through the questions we ask students as they work or at the end of a collaborative task. Responses to the questions can be communicated in a range of ways – visual, written, oral, dramatic, etc. The questions may be particularly helpful at the end of an activity during 'share time'. These questions include:

- How well do you think your group worked today?
- How do you know you/your group worked well?
- What is one thing you saw someone do or heard someone say that helped the group work well?

- What is one thing that you saw someone do or heard someone say that made it hard for your group to work well together?
- How did you feel when you were working in your group?
- How do you know when a group is working well?
- What does a good group look like? Feel like? Sound like?
- What was one thing you think you did really well to help your group?
- What is something you would like to do better next time?
- Why do you think it is a good idea to work in groups?
- How is it different to working by yourself?
- When do you like to work with others/alone? Why?
- What did you learn from working in a team?

These kinds of questions are designed to raise students' awareness of why they work this way, to raise the importance of each person's contribution and to improve their understanding of the processes involved.

Something to try

Strategy 1

Fishbowl

Fishbowl is particularly useful as a means of explicating the processes required for effective group work. It allows students to observe group interaction and to reflect on what they see.

Directions

1. Decide on a task to be completed by a small focus group. For example, the group may be set the task of brainstorming ideas about a topic, or coming to a consensus about a particular decision or plan – any task that involves a group working towards a shared goal or outcome.

2. Invite the remaining students to form a circle (sitting or standing) around the focus group.

3. Give students who are observing some guidelines/prompts such as the ones below and explain that they are to observe in silence.

   Sample prompts for fishbowl observations:
   - What do people do or say to help the group get the job done?
   - What got in the way of the group getting the job done well?
   - How do people solve problems when they arise?
   - How does people's body language affect the communication in the group?

4. Students in the observer roles then provide the group with feedback.

Adaptations/extensions

- Invite individuals from outside the fishbowl to come into the focus group (centre) and take the place of someone in the group to repeat the activity in a different way.

- Students take on a particular disposition or attitude during the task (for example, domineering or disinterested) and then discuss what effect this has on the group.

- Divide the class in half and have one half in the centre discussing an issue or topic while the others listen and observe. Then swap.

- Use 'fishbowling' incidentally. When you notice a group working particularly well, invite others to watch them (advise the group first).

- Ask one or more students to be 'secret' participant observers during class activity time and have them report back at the end of the session, noting the examples of great cooperative behaviour they saw during the session.

- Observers provide feedback in written form rather than orally.

Strategy 2

Group Freeze-frame

In this activity, groups of students must use their bodies to make a scene, model or structure to illustrate what they understand about effective teams. The guiding parameters are that each person must participate in the sculpture and that there is to be silence and stillness during the actual 'performance'. The group can decide on several contrasting or sequential scenes to perform.

Directions

1. Explain to students that they are going to create a sculpture or a scene using just their bodies. There is to be no movement or voice involved in the scene; it is like a 'frozen moment'. They should pay attention to their facial expression and the use of gestures and body positions to tell the story of the moment.

2. Give students a focus for their freeze-frame. It may be something connected to a current topic of study or a more general idea. For example:
   - An uncooperative/cooperative group
   - A bullying situation
   - A joyous occasion
   - A winning/losing moment

3. Give students time to rehearse their freeze-frame. They need to be able to move in and out of them quickly and silently.

4. Have each group perform their freeze-frame to others. The audience should be given an opportunity to interpret what they are seeing before the group explain their work.

5. Ask students to reflect on the way they worked during the activity. What did they find easy/fun/challenging, etc.?

Adaptations/extensions

- Each group creates a series of freeze-frames to show a sequence of events. The class close their eyes in between each one and opens them on a signal given by the group.

- Take digital photos of the freeze-frames, and have students create captions, thought bubbles or speech balloons to accompany them either on screen or on paper.

- Students can be asked to 'freeze' during any activity, and then to reflect on what their body language/positions say about the way the group is working.

Strategy 3

Silent Jigsaw

This activity works well with pairs or trios and helps students develop their non-verbal communication skills. The images chosen for the activity may relate in some way to a current topic being studied.

Directions

1. Select several pictures that are related in some way, for example a set of pictures of different beach environments, portraits of different people (using faces of the students is great fun) or different animals. The activity works well if the pictures have some similarities in their colour/design. Cut each image up into pieces and mix them up.

2. Group students. There should be the same number of students in the group as there are complete images. For example, a group of four students will be working with the mixed-up pieces of four images.
3. Distribute the pieces of the images evenly amongst the group members. Each student will now have a pile of pieces from different images.
4. Tell the students that they must now try to create one picture each, using their own and each other's pieces *in silence*.
5. Once the images have been created, the students should be asked to reflect on the task before discussing the images themselves. For example, they should identify that the key to success in this task is to help each other.

Adaptations/extensions

*   Combine the activity with a fishbowl observation strategy (see page 28).
*   A similar experience can be offered through collaborative constructions or drawings. Each student is given an equal number of construction components. They must take it in turns to add one component to a model to gradually create something. Alternatively, students can work in pairs or trios to create a shared drawing/diagram. Explain that it is to be one picture, planned and created by the team.

Strategy 4

Doing My Bit

It is important that individual students understand the way they can contribute to the success of a team. The Doing My Bit worksheet (page 34) is designed to help students identify and reflect on personal goals in relation to team work.

Directions

1. In groups or as a class, brainstorm the specific behaviours and skills that individuals can use to enhance the work of a team.
2. Ask individuals to organise this list (or the one on the worksheet) according to the behaviours/skills they feel most and least competent in.
3. Prior to collaborative tasks, ask individuals to use the worksheet to identify a goal for the session/duration of the task. This may or may not be discussed directly with the teacher and be the product of negotiation.
4. Once the task has been completed, students briefly reflect on their progress towards the goal and consider whether they need to continue to focus on this area or set a new goal.

Adaptations/extensions

*   Adapt the worksheet to provide peer feedback. Once students have identified a personal goal, the reflection section may be filled in by a peer who has been observing the student in action.

- Explore each element on the worksheet in more depth. Ask the class to identify what, for example, 'compromising' involves. Role-play examples of each one or list indicative behaviour.
- Use the worksheet as a checklist to record the progress of individual students in relation to cooperative learning behaviour.
- Video a group at work and then have them use the worksheet as a guide to observing their own behaviour in the video.
- Mirror/role-play some of these behaviours back to students (perhaps with another teacher) and ask them to tell you what you are doing and how this might affect the group.

SNAPSHOT

Using charts, images and posters to develop understandings about team work

Kath Gillick Maher

Kath had a class with many lively students who had some difficulties cooperating with others. She decided that she needed to be much more explicit about the collaborative process and that the students needed to have constant visual and verbal reminders to help them develop the necessary skills. To this end, Kath involved her students in designing posters and charts about various aspects of cooperation, displaying these around the room.

Kath and the students referred to the charts regularly to rehearse for or debrief after a collaborative activity. Digital images were taken while students were working together and these were shown to students to identify or analyse aspects of collaborative behaviour. Students added speech balloons to the photos, assisting them to think more carefully about the kind of dialogue that takes place in an effective group. Students began to refer to the posters and photos while they were working to remind each other what they needed to do.

MY WORKSHEET
Doing My Bit

Name: _____

GOALS	DATE	REFLECTION
Actively listen to others		
Use positive body language		
Give positive feedback to other group members		
Help the group stay on track and on task		
Wait my turn and don't talk over others		
Assert my opinion appropriately		
Help the group keep to time		
Make constructive suggestions		
Compromise		
Accept feedback/criticism of my ideas		

3   One size does not fit all
Engaging individual learners

Teaching and learning principles

- When students are emotionally involved in learning, they are more likely to stay on task, accept challenges and remain motivated.
- Challenge is important for engaging students.
- Each student learns differently. Teachers must cater for differences in interests, needs, backgrounds and learning styles.
- Learners are more engaged when they have some control and responsibility over their learning.
- Learning is more engaging when the learner perceives it to be personally relevant and useful in some way.
- Individual, constructive and ongoing feedback can be a powerful key to engaging the learner.
- The physical environment can have a significant impact on the learner's engagement.
- Teacher expectation has a profound impact on the way learners see their own potential.
- Students need sustained periods of time to maximise learning.

Introductory statement

There are many things that can be done at whole school and individual classroom level to ensure stronger engagement of more students. In effect, our efforts need to cast a wider net to avoid excluding and disadvantaging students who may not fit into the traditionally prescribed norms of student success.

Engaging students involves presenting and negotiating appropriately challenging tasks and differentiating our teaching to cater for individual differences. This requires teachers to have a sound knowledge of student abilities, interests and needs, and a broad repertoire of strategy ideas.

As well as understanding students individually, an understanding of the different ways that students learn is crucial. Reflecting on the range of ways that we, as teachers, like to learn can be enlightening. As much as we would like to, we cannot *make* our students learn, but we can establish a classroom climate, relationships and conditions that encourage students to become emotionally and cognitively involved in, and responsible for, their own learning. For example, providing sustained periods of time for planning, processing, reflecting on and assessing self-learning can increase motivation. Listening to student preferences and providing meaningful choices also engages students.

This chapter will explore ways to emotionally engage and challenge all learners by providing a range of experiences, ways for students to collect, process and present their own data, to be actively involved in their own learning, and to make some choices about what and how they will learn.

Making it happen: guidelines for engaging individuals

Build on prior knowledge and experiences

An obvious starting point for engaging students in the learning process is to start with the learner's prior knowledge and experiences. This is often done by teachers at the beginning of Year 7, particularly in terms of their families and what is important to students. Most teachers find out a bit about their students at the beginning of the year and may involve them in personal goal setting. This process of checking what students know, can do and are interested in is crucial for all aspects of learning, not just at the beginning of the year.

Things I know

I know Aboriginal kids were taken away from their mums a long time ago.

Things I want to find out

I would like to learn more about Corroborees.

When teachers identify and work from prior knowledge and experience, they are better able to take students beyond what they already know, rather than making assumptions about what they know or don't know. Time can be wasted repeating work already known or introducing work before students are ready. The effect of 'getting it wrong' (in terms of readiness) on self-esteem and motivation is hard to measure. It takes very little time to complete prior knowledge tasks and is worth the time. In addition to providing useful assessment data, students can learn from each other in the process and be motivated to learn more. Prior knowledge activities also reveal misconceptions about this and can help teachers attend more specifically to student needs. Some examples include concept mapping, brainstorming, bundling, student interviews, visualisation and prediction, freeze-framing and word and image associations.

Involving students in decision making

An extension of building on prior knowledge is to involve students in other decision-making processes related to their own learning. Self-assessment is a useful process to facilitate personal learning decision making. The following table provides a brief outline of what might be included in a goal setting planning sheet. It is important that goals are specific and achievable (see also the Personal Investigation Planner worksheet on page 49 and Chapter 4).

Teacher goals	
Student goals	
Time lines	
Indicators of success	
Teacher feedback	
Self-assessment	
Action plan	

Self-assessing and goal setting require practice. Students need to be given guidance about teacher expectations. Individual, constructive and ongoing feedback can be a powerful key to engaging the learner and developing responsible learners.

> **My goals**
>
> Keep my work organized and in a safe place.
> Let everyone have a fair and equal shot at working together.
> Don't over do my work.

Providing choices

Offering a variety of activities and strategies allows students a range of ways to perceive, process, communicate and evaluate their learning. This is important to show we value a diversity of ways students learn, for students' engagement and to demonstrate that we think it is important for them to be involved in the learning process.

Where possible, students can be involved in negotiating aspects of the curriculum. Even young students can be involved in selecting from a list of activities, and older students can be increasingly involved, from designing some tasks to planning and evaluating their own curriculum. By coupling self-assessment with curriculum choices, accountability and responsibility can be highlighted.

Accommodating individual strengths and preferences

Different students learn differently – they receive and process information in a variety of ways. We need to plan for ways that accommodate all students' ways of working. Offering choices can be useful but in itself does not necessarily cater for a variety of strengths, needs and learning preferences. However, an understanding of learning theories and current educational ideas (for example, multiple intelligences, learning styles and modalities, and teacher auditing processes) can help ensure choices and selections are varied and appropriate. We also need to understand the unique learning styles and preferences of each individual learner. When students develop an awareness of their own learning needs (see Chapter 1), they can make informed choices about ways to develop their own learning.

The following table provides an overview of how some theorists and educators have tried to organise thinking and learning to better cater for the range of learners in their classrooms. Any one of these could be used to assist planning and auditing learning experiences (refer to page 113 for full bibliographic details).

Multiple Intelligences (Gardner 1993)	Modalities (Coil 1999, adapted from Brandler-Grinder)	Whole brain learning – our four selves (Atkins 1993, adapted from Herrmann)	Learning styles (Gregorc-Butler in Guild and Garger 1985)
Verbal–linguistic Logical–mathematical Spatial Bodily–kinaesthetic Musical–rhythmic Naturalist Interpersonal Intrapersonal Spiritual	Visual Auditory Kinaesthetic Technological	**Left mode thinking** Rational theoretical (e.g. logical) Ordered, safekeeping (e.g. planned) **Right mode thinking** Imaginative experimental (e.g. holistic) Emotional interpersonal (e.g. intuitive)	Concrete sequential Abstract sequential Concrete random Abstract random

In addition, the following are worth remembering when planning to accommodate a range of learners in classrooms.

- Provide opportunities for students to participate in public performances, for example debates and role-plays.

- Allocate special time for helping students explore and articulate how they learn best (see McGrath and Noble 1995).
- Identify the interests and strengths of students, parents and others in the community and capitalise on these wherever possible.
- Allow students time to evaluate their learning choices.
- Students may be able to select and organise their own choices.
- Choose activities that involve a variety of senses, particularly touch, to cater better for the large number of kinaesthetic learners (who are least well catered for).

All students, including those with specific or other learning disabilities, have strengths, interests and learning preferences that will help facilitate their learning. It is our moral obligation to become informed enough about these to make a positive difference to all students' learning.

INDIVIDUAL LEARNING PLAN

Student's name: _____

Teacher: _____

Date: _____

REVIEW OF PROGRESS

Writing:
- Developing fine motor skills, improving legibility of handwriting.
- Confident to try different styles of writing.
- Using capital letters and full stops most of the time.
- Beginning to reread and recognise when meaning is lost.

Speaking and listening:
- Speaks clearly and thoughtfully, ensuring others understand.
- Listens carefully to instructions; beginning to ask questions when an instruction or activity is misunderstood.

Life skills:
- Usually responsible and able to resolve some small problems independently.
- Developing organisational skills; collecting resources prior to beginning; remaining on task to complete activities.

LEARNING IMPROVEMENT GOALS

Writing:
- To continue to develop fine motor skills, improving letter formation, spacing and size of handwriting.
- To develop writing skills across a range of unfamiliar topics/genres.
- To reread and revise own writing, identifying when meaning is lost or words are repeated or omitted.

Speaking and listening:
- To project voice and develop confidence when presenting work/reading.
- To ask questions for information/clarify concepts being taught, particularly when unsure.

Life skills:
- To remain on task for longer periods of time.
- To develop strategies to solve small social problems.
- To develop confidence in own abilities and take greater risks.

Creating challenge, emotional engagement and purpose

Many students are not challenged enough to keep them interested in school. Expecting and planning for a high level of intellectual engagement is foundational for motivation. In addition to curriculum choices, opportunities for extension, creativity and problem solving should be provided. It is necessary to include relevant, contemporary and controversial local and global issues in the programme that connect with student emotions. They should be moved, involved and vocal (see Chapter 4).

Teachers should plan open-ended, challenging questions and tasks. These should be relevant and issues- or problem-based where possible (see Chapter 7). Involvement in and with the community is explored in Chapter 4.

Time for student questions is invaluable, not only for assessment purposes. These can be used as a basis for student inquiries. When students identify questions based on their own interest motivation is naturally higher. Although this may not always be possible, choices and challenge within teacher programmes must be considered a high priority.

Art is a subject through which students can explore issues. Teachers can encourage students to use their art to communicate their feelings and understandings to others.

Physical environment

There is no doubt that the physical environment can influence students' interest in learning. Many primary classrooms are aesthetically exciting. They celebrate student work by displaying it on walls, windows and from the ceiling. They often have charts supporting work and independent learning, such as word lists and group statements that can be used in writing. Students can use these rather than asking the teacher for help. Pets and other living things can create a sense of homeliness, and furniture can be arranged to facilitate group and individual working areas (see also Chapter 2).

Montessori classrooms, for example, demonstrate child-friendly environments by displaying tasks on shelves, providing child-sized furniture, etc. Apart from improving the accessibility of resources, this also demonstrates to students their centrality to the learning process.

Something to try

Strategy 1

Here's the Answer, What's the Question?

This strategy has good novelty value, but is also useful for assessing the breadth of student knowledge. It is suitable for mixed abilities because there is no one right answer. It is also a chance for the creative student to excel and for the benefits of cooperative group work to be demonstrated. It is worth eliminating some types of questions, such as those where students are just required to fill the gap. For example, if the answer was 'white' the question should not be: The president of the United States lives in the _____ house.

Directions

1. Provide students with answers based, for example, on a concept such as change, multiplication, punctuation or gravity. Ideally, they should relate to a topic under investigation. The answers can be written on the board, supplied on strips of paper or sealed in an envelope.
2. In groups, students meet to discuss the questions that could lead to the answer.
3. Responses are shared. Creative and logical responses can be applauded.

Adaptations/extensions

- Supply some students with the same answers and have them work individually. They could then find others who have responded differently to them.
- Secretly provide different answers related to the same topic to various groups. They can then read out their questions to the class and challenge them to guess their answer.
- Have a competition to see who can get the most questions.
- Allocate different criteria for judging the quality of the questions. For example, the most creative or the simplest.

Strategy 2

Gather, Enhance, Communicate

This strategy is designed to promote the involvement of students in learning decisions. The Gather, Enhance, Communicate worksheet (page 47) provides space for teachers and students to negotiate aspects of the curriculum, increasing responsibility and engagement. This worksheet is for use during one of the initial lessons in a unit. Allow time to discuss the questions with students. Some negotiation might be required, for example if the teacher wants to focus student questions or extend student modes of presentation.

Directions

1. Teachers complete the first section of the worksheet (Gather) by listing the understandings or focus questions that they want students to achieve by the end of the unit (see the first adaptation on page 43).

Gather

Information about

- Health resources in our area.
- Current health issues in the media.
- Different perspectives about health resource allocation.

Enhance

By posing your own questions

- How do governments decide what health issues are important?

- What if there is a health emergency?
- Do all get the same amount of money to spend on health?

Communicate

Your learning to others by

poster	de Bono's strategy
oral presentation ✓	role-play
concept map	collages
construction	graphic representation
report ✓	your idea

---

2   Students complete the Enhance section individually after some group discussion time.

3   Students also complete the Communicate section. This can occur after students have collected some information as some modes of presentation are better suited to particular data. Teachers may wish to direct students to a particular mode, such as visual mode.

Adaptations/extensions

- Allow students to complete the Gather section. Students define the information they want to collect. This requires some experience and teacher direction, as students may not know about aspects of the study that would be useful information.
- To involve students in the assessment process, they write what they learnt about the topic and the learning process on the back of the worksheet.
- Involve students in determining the criteria they use to make judgements about the quality of their own work. This is more achievable if students have had assessment criteria made explicit to them in the past, and if they have been involved in some form of either self-, peer or group assessment.

Strategy 3

What Would You Do?

This strategy is effective for exploring the impact of learnt information and for values clarification. It engages students because it involves values, feelings and emotions. It is an effective way of covering controversial topics. For example: The school playground should be turned into a car park for commuters.

Rules of courtesy and procedure need to be explained first. For example: only the person being interviewed by the teacher can speak; there is no one right answer; any argument is possible if it can be justified; no sexist or racist comments are allowed.

Directions

1. Read out a short scenario (a scenario related to the current topic is best). Students then stand along a line to show how they would react. The positions marked on the line are: Do nothing, Not sure, Do something.
2. Rove along the line and ask students at different positions to explain their choice.
3. Another scenario is read out and students can move places along the line if they wish.

Adaptations/extensions

- Remove the 'Not sure' category to force students to take a stand.
- Alternative positions could be included. For example: What do you believe?, True, False, What would you say?, Submissive, Aggressive, Assertive.
- If performed as a written task, have students compare their ideas with others, as much of its value is in hearing other people's perspectives.
- Instead of having the whole class physically moving positions, try a portion of the class at a time. The audience is not allowed to speak.
- Students can change positions after they have heard another student speak.

Strategy 4

Same But Different

This strategy asks students to develop their own ideas and then to actively seek out others who have different opinions. It aims to broaden student perspectives, to promote logical argument development and creative thinking.

Directions

1. Students are given a statement about an aspect of their studies in the content areas (Science, Design & Technology or PSHE). This is effective for teasing out contentious issues such as pollution, immigration, school uniforms or homework.
2. Students decide on their position by jotting down their major ideas (see the sample layout shown below).

My ideas	Someone else's ideas
How are our ideas similar?	**How are our ideas different?**

3. They then find someone in the room who has an alternative point of view. They summarise their views as well.
4. Ask students to synthesise the arguments according to how they are similar and how they are different.

Adaptations/extensions

*   Students try to convince someone else that their idea is right.
*   Students try to convince a third party of their partner's ideas (different to their own).
*   Students attempt to synthesise both arguments to create a new one. A Venn diagram could be used for this purpose.
*   Someone could collate all class responses and organise them into categories or along a continuum of ideas, for example from conservative to radical or logical to creative.

Strategy 5

Doing It My Way

The Doing It My Way worksheet (see page 48) is designed to help students plan their own learning adventure. It provides prompts, suggestions and directions for them to follow so that they can choose what they learn and how they represent that learning.

Directions

Explain the purpose of each part of the worksheet, providing examples if necessary.

Adaptations/extensions

- Partially complete the worksheet so that it is less negotiable. For example, create a limited list for students to choose from or specify exactly what they will be learning so they have no choice.
- Negotiate with each individual what they will learn and/or the way they represent their learning.
- Use the ideas on the sheet for many purposes when students have a choice of methods to represent their learning.

SNAPSHOT

Multi-modal contract

Rebecca Walsh

Rebecca is a beginning teacher who wanted to challenge all learners and cater for the range of learning needs and strengths of her students. She had some students who were sometimes reluctant, and Rebecca wanted to provide learning choices and to develop skills for learning independently. To do this Rebecca decided to create a contract sheet to help process information gathered about the integrated curriculum topic on marine life. She designed four activities for each of the learning modes: visual, auditory and kinaesthetic. The contract was introduced to the students with the assistance of support teachers.

Students were given a worksheet with activity choices on it. The worksheet had space for teacher comments and for students to record when they started and finished an activity. Students completed as many activities as possible in a six-week period. At the end of this time students were asked to present their work to the rest of the class for peer assessment. They took the peer assessment task very seriously. Students were also required to self-assess their work using an extensive rubric designed by Rebecca. The students really enjoyed the contracts and were disappointed when the contract time ended.

Marine animals video activities

Name:_____

You may choose and complete **three** activities from the following list. You must choose one activity from each section and have a teacher approve the activities you choose before you start. These activities need to show what you have learnt about marine environments.

Activities	What I would like to do	Date started	Date finished	Teacher's comments
AUDITORY				
In a group, role-play different groups involved in conservation of the sea.				
Write a piece of poetry about marine animals.				
Compose a song or piece of music about marine animals.				
Write an argument about why we need to look after the sea.				
VISUAL				
Make a list of questions that you will email to an expert.				
Create a poster showing why and how we can look after the sea.				
Draw a food chain showing all the marine animals you know.				
Write a letter to a conservation expert. Ask questions about, or make suggestions on, how we can look after the marine environment.				
KINAESTHETIC				
Make a diorama or model showing the marine life you know and anything you may have learnt from the video.				
Design and make a board game that creates awareness about marine environments and how humans have changed them.				
Make a mobile showing all the marine animals you know and how humans have changed the marine environment.				
Make a data or fact chart that shows what you have learnt and what you would like to learn about marine environments.				
Make a factual picture book about marine environments and how humans have changed them that can be read to a Year 1/2 class.				
Make a flip book that shows how humans have changed the marine environment.				

MY WORKSHEET
Gather, Enhance, Communicate

Name: _____

GATHER

. . . information about

-
-
-
-

ENHANCE

. . . by posing your own questions

-
-
-
-

COMMUNICATE

. . . your learning to others by (one of the following)

1. poster	2. letter
3. oral presentation	4. role-play
5. concept map	6. collage
7. construction	8. graphic representation
9. report	10. your idea

MY WORKSHEET
Doing It My Way

Name: _____

---

1. I want to learn about . . .
(knowledge)

2. I want to learn to . . .
(skills)

4. Due date: _____

Signature:

_____

Teacher signature:

_____

Parent signature:

_____

5. Teacher comment:

---

3. I have chosen to show my learning by . . .

- ☐ Listing fascinating facts
- ☐ Writing a newspaper report
- ☐ Writing a letter
- ☐ Tape recording
- ☐ Video recording
- ☐ Creating a rap, rhyme or song
- ☐ Writing a poem
- ☐ Writing a reflective journal entry
- ☐ Creating true and false questions
- ☐ Designing a chat-show interview
- ☐ Making up a metaphor
- ☐ Designing a cause and effect wheel
- ☐ Painting or drawing
- ☐ Making a mobile
- ☐ Creating a diorama
- ☐ Writing a play or puppet show
- ☐ Drawing a flow chart
- ☐ Writing a recipe
- ☐ Designing an advertisement
- ☐ Making a poster/mural
- ☐ Drawing a story map
- ☐ Drawing a cartoon strip
- ☐ Creating an instruction manual
- ☐ Making up a 'What am I?' quiz
- ☐ Creating a Venn diagram
- ☐ Writing a glossary of new words
- ☐ Graphing major findings
- ☐ Making up a game
- ☐ Drawing contrasting images
- ☐ Writing a pledge
- ☐ Defining key words or ideas using symbols

Personalised Learning in the Primary Classroom © Kath Murdoch and Jeni Wilson, Routledge, 2008

MY WORKSHEET
Personal Investigation Planner

Name: _____

? **What are my questions? What do I want to find out about?**

How will I find out about this? (tick the box)

☐ Talking to people

☐ Reading books

☐ Using the computer

☐ Going somewhere

☐ Watching video/DVD

☐ Other (draw your own)

How will I show what I know?

☐ Drawing or painting

☐ Writing

☐ Talk

☐ Use the computer

☐ Acting

☐ Music/song

☐ Making a model

When will I be ready to share? (write a date) _____

Signed: _____ (student)

Signed: _____ (parent)

Personalised Learning in the Primary Classroom © Kath Murdoch and Jeni Wilson, Routledge, 2008

4 Making the world of difference
Establishing wider community connections

Teaching and learning principles

- Authentic, real-life learning experiences can promote high levels of engagement.
- Learners need a sense of purpose to guide and motivate their learning.
- Families and communities are important sources of knowledge and skills that can enrich the school curriculum.
- Students benefit from interacting with a range of people as they learn – not just teachers.
- Close partnerships between home and school are beneficial for students.
- Involvement in action projects develops important skills for lifelong learning.
- Schools can enhance communities through shared, authentic projects.

Introductory statement

Increasingly, school education is viewed as an opportunity to develop skills, qualities and understandings that will enable students to become active citizens within local and global contexts. Schools are unique organisations. They are a community within themselves – students, parents, teachers and others, and existing within them are several smaller communities of students in classes. These form an interconnected web of people with various skills, roles, rights and responsibilities.

Schools are also at the heart of a wider community. This is particularly true in remote or rural areas, where they can be a meeting place or a centre of activity, especially in difficult times. Schools are well positioned to offer students real experiences of active citizenship both within the organisation itself and across the local and global communities beyond the school. In this chapter, we will explore guidelines and strategies for enhancing the opportunities for authentic, 'community connections' for students – both within and beyond the school.

Becoming more active and productive citizens is a compelling reason to create community-based opportunities for students. However, there are numerous other benefits for students. By being involved in real issues and activities within the school and wider community, students are given a wonderful context to develop some of the most essential skills, qualities and understandings of the lifelong learner. Authentic projects can help 'blur' the distinction between learning in and learning beyond the school.

The upper primary and lower secondary years of schooling, in particular, are described as a time when many students become disengaged from their learning. One of the key strategies to address this problem is to build a stronger emphasis on parental and community involvement in student learning and to provide learning experiences that students see as meaningful, relevant, practical and problem based. Involving students in issues and activities directly related to the school and/or local and global communities is a powerful way to address the problem of disengagement and alienation. Through this approach, students can be positioned to take on more responsibility, make real decisions, plan and organise, and work collaboratively. They may also experience a greater sense of satisfaction and achievement for having solved a problem or contributed to the creation of something worthwhile for themselves and others. Seeing our students involved in authentic, real-life projects also gives us an opportunity to find out more about them; to see the ways they interact and to assess key skills and qualities such as communication, cooperation, persistence and flexibility.

Making it happen: guidelines for community connections

Get to know the local community

As teachers, we should ask ourselves: What do I really know about the community in which I work? What 'lens' do I view this community through? Who are the significant people in this community? What are the issues that matter to the families with whom I work? Teachers and students do not always live in the area in which they go to school. Understanding the characteristics, history and general profile of the local area can help teachers use and connect with the community more effectively. Misconceptions about the culture and identity of a community and the people within it often develop as part of the 'staffroom mythology'. The assumptions or judgements that we often make too quickly about people and places should be challenged, as they can have a significant impact on the way we design the curriculum for our students.

Visiting community venues (such as the local health centre, preschool or youth centre), talking with local council workers and walking around the local area are useful activities to experience as a whole staff. Teachers who do live in the area should be encouraged to share their perspectives with others. Exploring the local community through the eyes of students, parents and grandparents can also be a powerful and informative exercise, helping develop a better understanding of both the needs of the community and the resources it can provide to the school. Local newspapers and the local government offices can be a valuable, regular source of information – not only about the community in general, but about issues and events affecting it. These issues may then become opportunities for student inquiry or problem-based learning.

Involve students in decisions about the school, their class and their learning

Many wonderful opportunities for authentic and issues-based learning are right in front of us and yet are too often overlooked. These opportunities are in the form of everyday decisions and actions that are part of the life of a school (such as dealing with a litter problem or designing a new playground). Ironically, the very people who will be most affected by these decisions and actions – the students – are not often involved in the process. Involving students in decision making about the school begins in the classroom. By participating in decisions about class protocol, responsibilities, routines and furniture arrangements we can apprentice students into the skills and processes required in community decision making beyond the classroom. At a whole school level, decisions and issues such as those listed below offer opportunities for active engagement, real-life learning and an enhanced sense of belonging and ownership amongst students. The degree of responsibility students are given within these contexts will depend on many factors, such as the age of the students, but every student can make some contribution to at least one aspect of the daily life of their school.

Ideas for school-based inquiry projects

- Establish and monitor environmental systems in the school, such as recycling, waste management systems or energy efficiency measures.
- Participate in school and community forums on various issues.
- Develop policies and practices with students relating to equity and justice issues, such as gender equity or sport.
- Develop a code of conduct with students that is clear and explicit and used across the school.
- Review the food sold in the canteen in terms of its nutrition value.
- Design new uniforms, school logos or mottos.
- Create advertising brochures or posters to promote the school.
- Organise major events, such as a school fete, sports day, graduation or grandparents day.
- Plan to build or renovate school buildings.
- Organise exhibitions and open days.
- Cater for and organise functions for parents or community members, such as an Information Night.
- Purchase sports equipment (students can be involved in decisions about needs analysis, surveys, costing, budgeting, ordering, storing, etc.).
- Develop awards and other forms of recognising achievement.

Inquiry projects have the potential to give students a sense of real purpose in their learning. However, it remains the task of the strategic teacher to make these purposes explicit. Action projects become better vehicles for understandings when we can identify the concepts or 'big ideas' embedded in them. For example, planting and maintaining a school garden not only develops understandings about living things, survival and growth, but also about the nature of work, sustainability, decision making and enterprise. Action projects should be selected and designed carefully. The following questions can help teachers consider the value of a possible project:

- Have the students themselves indicated that they are concerned about this issue? Do they see it as important?
- Are there opportunities for students to communicate how they feel or what they believe about the issue?
- Are there resources (human and other) that can be accessed by students to find out more about the issue?
- Does the issue itself have 'generative potential' for linking to big ideas about the world? That is, will it teach students more about things such as change, interdependence, systems, connectedness and diversity?
- Will students be able to see some kind of change (however small) as a result of their actions?
- Have the consequences of actions on others or the environment been well considered?

(See the Planning for Action worksheet on page 62.)

Keep a collective 'finger on the pulse' (local and global)

Issues that arise from local and global events can be the springboard to the most exciting and worthwhile teaching opportunities. Students and staff should be encouraged to maintain their awareness of what's going on in the world around them and to share information and discoveries with others. One of the most obvious ways of doing this is to subscribe to a daily newspaper (either print or online). Topics or units being covered by different classes should be made public so that others can identify current events and related resources. Bulletin boards, newsletters, websites and other shared media can be used as a forum to report on or raise issues about local and global issues. Importantly, time should be given in class to allow students to discuss, process, respond to and reflect on issues arising in their local and global communities. Even very young students have exposure to media coverage of events that may be well beyond their capacity to understand. We may underestimate the effect of their exposure to such issues. Being sensitive to this as teachers and providing opportunities for open discussion and response are an important part of ensuring our schools maintain links with the world beyond.

Foster strong partnerships with parents/caregivers and the community

We firmly believe that when teachers and parents work together, students' learning improves. Schools that create an inviting, participatory culture and actively promote parent involvement at all levels can be dynamic and strongly 'connected' places. There are a myriad of ways in which parental participation can be manifested in a school.

Importantly, the participation of parents should be seen not just as an opportunity to enhance the education of the student, but as a potential resource to benefit the whole school. Grandparents and friends are also often an untapped resource with, perhaps, more time and skills that can be of great value to support the work of teachers. Tapping into expertise beyond the school can be a vital component of successful teaching and learning. As part of the inquiry process, we encourage teachers to 'bring in the experts' so students can find out about a topic from a direct and authentic source. If young students are inquiring into gardens with a view to planting one in the school grounds, invite a gardener to answer their questions. Students finding out about endangered species may question a zoologist. The power of learning from someone with a real passion and expertise in a field is clear, even with very young learners.

Seize the moment

While we advocate a well planned and long-term 'map' of curriculum (see Chapter 7), we also maintain the importance of 'the spontaneous moment' as a powerful vehicle for teaching and learning. Overly restrictive structures and routines can hamper the spontaneity that creates some of the most memorable teaching and learning moments. It is in the area of community connections that such spontaneous moments often occur. Teachers need to feel that they have 'permission' to respond to local or global events and issues, and to use these as a basis for teaching and learning activities. Obviously, there is always something going on in the world around us, but we argue that teachers are very astute when it comes to identifying issues or events that they believe will capture students' hearts and minds, as well as provide powerful opportunities for learning.

Devastating events, such as September 11, the Bali bombings and the war in Iraq, challenge teachers to deal with students' questions and reactions appropriately. Alongside such horrific events, there continue to be powerful, positive moments such as lives saved through acts of great bravery. The students we teach today have a far greater awareness of such events, and we have a responsibility to help them make sense of what they see and hear – to critique and respond to it. To do otherwise is denying our students an important opportunity not only to process and express their feelings, but to learn more about the way the world works. Importantly, these issues help students explore the range of perspectives and values held by people across the globe, as well as within the classroom.

Commit to making a difference

One of the ways we can teach students about positive, active citizenship is through modelling. Many schools make contributions through fundraising, sponsoring or volunteer work to community organisations, charities or similar. This can take the form of a short-term appeal or a long-term partnership. Environmental, social or health-related organisations can provide the perfect vehicle for showing students the role they can play in improving the quality of their lives now and in the future. They also provide a context for developing skills and understandings about enhancing the quality of life for others. It can also be a powerful and unifying experience for school staff, and one that can involve the whole community. Special days or celebrations can be organised to raise awareness (and possibly funds!).

There are many organisations that welcome the involvement of schools. Students should be highly involved in the processes of finding out about the organisations, selecting and corresponding with them, and monitoring the results of any actions or contributions they make. Some examples of these organisations include Oxfam, UNICEF, Greenpeace, the British Red Cross and the Royal Society for the Protection of Birds.

Something to try

Strategy 1

Need a Hand?

Finding out and recording the skills and expertise of each student creates a strong sense of community, and leads to the understanding that a community is made up of different people who play different roles. Students also become more aware of how they can support and be supported by other class members, reducing dependence on the teacher.

Directions

1. Discuss the idea of a skills directory with students. Find out what they know about directories. Students in the early years may need to examine some examples such as telephone directories, local council information booklets, school staff directories and computer databases.

2. Explain that you are going to create a class directory. Ask students: What features would this directory have? What will need to be included? How could the directory be presented? What information do you want to include in the directory?

3. Time may need to be spent discussing the kinds of skills and knowledge that could be included in the directory. Encourage students to think beyond school into areas of expertise they have developed in their home lives and so on.

4. Once you have decided on the content and format, students work individually or in groups to gather and record the information.

Name	Class	Can help others learn how to	Can help others learn about	Additional information
Daniel Ray	6B	Use computer programs	Plants and animals	Can also do good drawings

Adaptations/extensions

- Include information from parents or people from the wider community. Older students may be given the responsibility of creating and maintaining a school-wide directory accessible to all students.
- Record and present the data in the style of a telephone directory, on a set of indexed cards or digital database.
- This activity can be developed as part of the literacy programme as it requires digital literacy skills, and recording and organising information in different ways.
- Feature one expert per week in the school or classroom. The expert can be interviewed by other students, have their photos displayed and be written up in the newsletter.

Strategy 2

What's the Matter?

This activity provides a method for finding out what students are interested in and concerned about in relation to themselves and the world around them. It is an adaptation of James Beane's (1997) negotiated curriculum model and incorporates the skill of bundling or classifying ideas.

Directions

1. What's happening? Students identify questions or issues of concern they have in relation to their local or global community. Individuals can brainstorm these on a concentric circles diagram as below:

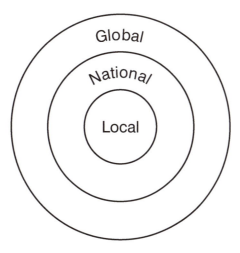

2. After their initial brainstorm, students create a question from each idea. Each question is written on a separate card. For example, 'Not enough for young people to do in our neighbourhood', becomes:

> How can the local area provide more things for kids to do in their spare time?

3. In small groups, students share their questions and then bundle them into piles of questions with a common theme/idea.
4. Repeat step 3 in larger groups. Two small groups come together and bundle their questions.
5. As a class, make a list of some of the most common issues/questions that were identified by groups. List the issues in question form as they can become the basis of a shared, problem-based inquiry later on (see Chapter 7).

Adaptations/extensions

- Provide a higher-level thinking challenge. Number each of the questions on the class list. Ask each student to decide the order of priority they would put the questions into. Have students compare their prioritised lists and discuss similarities and differences.

- Students consider ways that the questions could be investigated. Ask: What topics would help us find out more about this?
- Use the questions as the basis of simple mind maps to explore what students currently think about the issues.
- Students share the results of the activity with their parents and ask what they would consider to be the most important questions.
- Display the questions in the classroom and have students find articles or images that link to each one.
- Students list their questions in the school newsletter and ask for experts or relevant community speakers to come in and talk with them about the issues of most importance.

Strategy 3

Get the Picture?

This strategy is designed to encourage students to think about a range of real-life events and issues using current affairs described in newspapers, magazines, websites, picture sets, etc. Working with images helps students critically analyse visual texts. By selecting images that relate to significant issues, the strategy encourages important dialogue that can lead to ideas for action. Through their interaction with the texts, you will also gain an insight into the level of awareness and understanding students have about the events and issues in the world around them.

Directions

1. Students go through the daily newspaper and cut out images used to accompany a range of stories. Select a representative sample of images from the collection they have gathered.
2. Have students rank the images according to:
   - how they make them feel (such as, from good to bad or comfortable to uncomfortable)
   - how important the related issues are to them
   - how relevant they are to their own lives and experiences.
3. Discuss the similarities and differences between the responses.
4. In small groups, students analyse one of the images and create a caption that might have appeared in the newspaper.

Adaptations/extensions

- Use the Get the Picture worksheet (page 61) to create a 'lucky dip' of cards. In groups, students take it in turns to pick out a card and then analyse the picture using that particular question.
- Students select one image and write a brief statement to describe what is

happening in it. They draw one picture to show what they think might have happened before the photograph was taken and then another picture to show what might have happened afterwards. Compare these to the actual events reported in the articles.

- Students select an image and write what they think the image is about, how it makes them feel and/or what it reminds them of before reading the accompanying text.
- Students 'put themselves in the picture'. Where would they be? What would they be doing? How would they be feeling?

Strategy 4

Planning for Action

As part of a unit of work or in response to a particular issue/need, students can create personal or small group action projects. Involving students in planning an action project is a powerful way to teach skills of time management, research, team work, communication and organisation. It can also provide students with a feeling of satisfaction and connectedness through achieving a real outcome.

Directions

1. This strategy usually extends over several sessions. Initially, a whole class brainstorm of suitable projects can help students develop their ideas (these may be based on the issues arising from the What's the Matter? strategy, page 56).
2. Model or jointly construct a sample planner with the whole class. Think aloud to identify the kinds of questions students should consider when they are planning.
3. Encourage students to form small groups to plan their projects. Groups can use the Planning for Action worksheet (page 62) to draft an overview of their plan.
4. Meet with each group to discuss their plan and to make suggestions for improvement. Have groups meet with each other to provide peer feedback on their project plan.
5. Once students are working through their planned project, allow several opportunities for a progress report. Students should also reflect on the project upon completion.

Adaptations/extensions

- Adapt the worksheet format for use as a whole class or individual planner.
- Adapt the process to work on small school-based projects or global projects.
- Develop a rubric with students to help identify the features of an effective action project.

SNAPSHOT

Using real issues for project-based learning

Karen Richardson, Jo Schwartz, Colleen Holloway and Gill Aulich

The building of a new school prompted a team of teachers to plan innovative project-based units of work exploring the key question: What kind of school community do we want?

They developed a focused inquiry around the topic of student leadership. The head teacher asked students to prepare a proposal for student leadership structures and roles in the new school. Working towards this, students embarked on investigations of leadership structures in other schools as well as in the wider community. They interviewed people, surveyed other students, gathered data about the needs of staff and students and analysed the data in order to develop a draft proposal. The proposal was then put to the head teacher and a forum of Year 9 students, followed by a series of meetings between the head teacher and a small committee of students to finalise the plan.

'This was a very real project,' said the teachers involved. 'Initially, many of the students looked to their teachers for answers, but they gradually became more independent in their learning. They were certainly engaged in higher-order thinking – analysing, creating and evaluating. Being involved in a real-life project helped students see that they could make a difference and that their views would be listened to.' Feedback from students indicated that this was some-thing they valued highly. One student commented, 'I like being listened to and knowing that my opinion counts.'

SNAPSHOT

Taking action in and for the local community

Sarah Cuthbertson

The students in Sarah Cuthbertson's class became intrigued as to why their community did not have any recycling facilities. When they approached their local council they were informed that the cost of recycling was too great. This response did not sit well with them, and prompted a fascinating inquiry into recycling and composting. The class generated a survey to ask family members about waste and recycling and then tallied and graphed the data. They followed this by using a range of thinking strategies to come up with ideas on how to manage the waste problem. They then visited places such as paper mills and other related industries. Letters were sent to relevant people, outlining the data they had collected and proposing some possible solutions. Within a month, the children were visited by an industry representative who was very impressed with the detail and depth of their thinking. He announced that a recycling station, comprising six wheelie bins to collect glass, cans and plastics, would be installed by the end of that week. As the head teacher of the school noted, 'The students' learning has been based around putting actions into place – doing something about it!'

Get the Picture

What is happening in this picture? How do you know?	What caption would you give this image?	Imagine a photograph had been taken a few minutes before this one. What might it show?
Imagine a photograph had been taken a few minutes after this one. What might it show?	Who might have taken this photograph? Why? Where might the photograph be published?	How does this photograph 'work on you'? What effect is it intended to have on you? How has it been composed to achieve this?
What/who is not included in this photograph? Who/what could be present and is excluded/silent?	What might lie beyond the frame? If you could see beyond this image, what would you see?	If you could ask the person/people in this image some questions, what would you ask?
How are you like the person/people in this photo. Is there anything about you, your life or your experience that connects to this photo?	How does this image make you feel? Why?	What other images/events does this image remind you of?

Personalised Learning in the Primary Classroom © Kath Murdoch and Jeni Wilson, Routledge, 2008

MY WORKSHEET
Planning for Action

Name: _____

1. What do you hope to achieve through this action project? What are your goals?

   _____

2. Why is this important to you?

   _____

3. How will this project make a difference to your life or to other people?

   _____

4. What steps do you intend to take to work towards your goal? Who will be responsible for these tasks?

What needs to be done?	Who will do it?	When will it be completed?

5. What resources will you use to assist you with this project?

   _____

Reviewed by (teacher): _____ Date: _____

Reviewed by (peer): _____ Date: _____

To be completed by (date): _____

Personalised Learning in the Primary Classroom © Kath Murdoch and Jeni Wilson, Routledge, 2008

Menu of learning strategies

When planning units of work, use this menu to remind yourself of the strategies you can include as well as highlighting or checking the strategies used over time. These strategies should also be explicitly taught to students. Some strategies are outlined in this book, but teachers are encouraged to develop a menu that suits the needs of their students.

Strategies for developing thinking skills	Visual organisers
☐ Brainstorming	☐ Y charts
☐ Predicting/confirming	☐ Flow charts
☐ Bundling	☐ Data charts
☐ de Bono's 6 thinking hats	☐ Concept maps
☐ Thinkers' keys/thinking gears	☐ Spider diagrams
☐ Debates	☐ Mind maps
☐ Where do you stand?	☐ Cluster webs/tree diagrams
☐ Diamond ranking	☐ Effects wheels
☐ Self-assessment	☐ T-charts
☐ Journals (whole class/individuals)	☐ Labelled diagrams
☐ Goal setting and reflection	☐ Venn diagrams
	☐ Fishbone

Strategies for working collaboratively	Investigating/communicating through technology
☐ Think, pair, share	☐ PowerPoint
☐ 1–3–6 consensus	☐ Kid Pix
☐ Using specific roles	☐ Inspiration
☐ Jigsaw (expert groups)	☐ Making a web page
☐ Cross-age groups	☐ Electronic data chart (Excel)
☐ Peer assessment	☐ Making videos
☐ Fishbowl observations	☐ Digital photos
	☐ Multimedia presentations
	☐ Animations
	☐ Word documents
	☐ Audio tapes

Strategies/resources for investigation

☐ Question matrix
☐ Where/what/who/when/why/how starters
☐ Surveys/interviews
☐ Direct experiences (excursions)
☐ Learning from experts
☐ Internet
☐ CD-ROMs
☐ Experiments
☐ Film/video/TV
☐ Printed text
☐ Visual images
☐ Structured observations (fishbowling)
☐ Simulation
☐ Audio texts (music/songs)
☐ Email
☐ Fax/phone
☐ Letter
☐ Play-based explorations

5 Pressing the pause button
Teaching thinking strategically

> **Teaching and learning principles**
> - Reflection and metacognition are central to teaching and learning.
> - Students think in different ways. This should be valued and reflected in the teaching programme.
> - Reflective thinking and metacognition enhance students' responsibility for learning.
> - When students reflect on their own learning, they can select appropriate strategies, and set and act on their own goals.
> - When reflective thinking is valued and practised, student metacognition improves.
> - Thinking skills can be taught. This is best done within the context of meaningful content and purposeful activities.
> - Cooperative group work can enhance thinking.

Introductory statement

Metacognition is when a learner is aware of, evaluates and regulates their own thinking. Metacognition is promoted as crucial for learning because it involves active self-assessment and decision making, and personal goal setting. Involving students in their own thinking and learning in these ways is an important educational goal. Developing the capacity to think for themselves by using a variety of thinking skills is critical to becoming successful lifelong learners.

Reflective thinking is also promoted as important for learning but this is not the same as metacognition. Reflective thinking is about something other than one's own thinking. It is deeper than just thinking about something – it often raises questions, can be associated with problems and usually involves analysis and making judgements. Reflection and metacognition are keys to learning.

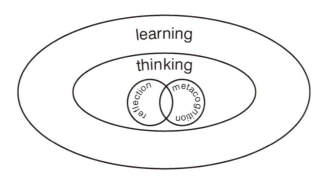

We learn from reflecting on experiences, feelings and beliefs. This is true for all learners, therefore we need to strategically plan and teach for thinking in the context of authentic, learner-centred classrooms regardless of the age or subject area.

In addition to understanding the importance of thinking, we also now recognise that different learners have different thinking preferences. Generally speaking, students who have a left-brain thinking preference feel more comfortable, capable and competent with critical thinking when they can examine, reason, organise, analyse, predict and hypothesise. Students who have a right-brain thinking preference feel more confident with creative thinking situations when they can generate new ideas, find, explore and consider options and alternatives.

Each of us uses both sides of our brain, but we often have a preferred way of thinking unless we are challenged. Using a range of thinking skills and strategies can extend students beyond their comfort zone. Working in non-preferred ways and with others with different thinking preferences and dispositions can be very powerful learning contexts. Such situations are likely to challenge students' thinking and engage them more fully in learning.

Organising learning to extend thinking requires teachers to have a sound knowledge of student abilities, skills, learning preferences, interests and needs. Understanding types of thinking skills and knowing strategies to enhance these skills can also create more thoughtful curricula.

A focus on thinking means we need to make time to 'press the pause button' – to ensure that students reflect all the way through the learning experience, not just at the end.

Making it happen: guidelines for thinking

Thinking should be an integral part of teaching and learning

Teachers are becoming more familiar with various thinking tools (such as de Bono's strategies), but these should not be taught in isolation. While we need to teach thinking skills explicitly, we also need to ensure that these skills are used in purposeful, contextualised ways.

Students should be learning to think about something worthwhile and draw upon different thinking skills and strategies. For example, at the start of a unit or lesson, teachers could ask students to identify their prior knowledge. Contradictions and beliefs could be identified (reflection and critical thinking) and self-assessed (metacognition). As the session/unit progresses, students can be asked to reflect on their changing ideas, develop new ideas/solutions (creative thinking) to consider the knowledge in light of their prior knowledge and to reflect on their own thinking (metacognition).

Opportunities can be planned for students to present their thinking in a variety of ways. Graphic organisers, for example, can be used to display thinking (see the Making Thinking Visual with Graphic Organisers worksheet on page 77). Other methods should be made available to cater for students who prefer to display their ideas in a more physical way, such as freeze-framing (see the At a Glance Thinking Guide on page 69).

Definitions

Skills are used to participate in learning (and life) tasks. They can be generic or context specific, but always relate to process. They include physical or mental skills. Put simply, they help get the job done. They are not the same as knowledge, but are often used to gain or sort knowledge. For example, a thinking skill is synthesising. When students use this skill, they are synthesising their own ideas and knowledge collected. Skills are **not** the same as strategies.

Strategies are similar to techniques (often these words are used interchangeably). They are similar to activities, but are usually broad and can therefore often be used in several contexts. Strategies usually involve students using more than one skill. For example, de Bono's hats are a strategy to help students think (use a range of thinking skills) about content (knowledge). Strategies are **not** the same as skills, knowledge or personal dispositions.

Dispositions (or personal qualities) such as being curious, empathetic and open minded are **not** the same as skills. However, dispositions can be encouraged or modelled through various strategies.

Strategic teacher planning for thinking

When planning to develop thinking within the classroom programme, the focus must be on the thinking type and/or skill required. This is determined by the needs of students and relates to the appropriate intellectual challenge for students in the class. While a variety of strategies is advantageous, the choice of strategy should not precede the purpose. We want students to be selective decision makers and we need to be too. The strategy must be selected to suit the purposes at the time. No matter how fashionable a strategy, if it is not appropriate to the context it could be a waste of time and cause student confusion over the purpose. The following provides the basis for a strategic thinking plan:

Strategic thinking plan

1. Focus on the thinking type and/or skill required.
   - Select one or more strategy to suit the purpose.
   - Ensure the strategy suits the context/material explored.
2. Check: Essential?
   - Does it suit the overall existing classroom planning?
   - Do students need direct, explicit instruction to be able to use the strategy?
   - Does it support or extend (not restrict) student thinking?
   - Are all students able to demonstrate what they think?

   Check: Useful?
   - Is the strategy open ended?
   - Is the strategy flexible enough to cater for all sorts of thinkers?
   - Istherepotentialforstudentstoadaptthestrategyiftheyneed/wantto?
3. Use the outcome for authentic assessment purposes.

Matching the strategy to the desired thinking engages students in this type of thinking. When students use creative thinking in one context, they will not necessarily become more creative (or reflective and critical) in all other situations. All skills, including thinking, require practice. They require regular revisiting within appropriate contexts. However, when students engage in a particular type of thinking or strategy, they have the opportunity to practise the skill, use the language, and think about and communicate their understandings of the process. Repeated, meaningful and explicit use of thinking skills and strategies should develop a better awareness of their own thinking.

We do not consider it necessary to develop a structured scope and sequence of thinking skills and strategies. Many of the skills and strategies needed for effective thinking are required by students regardless of their age/year level. To suggest we 'hold off' teaching a strategy because it is not in that year's scope and sequence could be unnecessarily prohibitive. Put bluntly, the random selection of thinking skills and strategies makes little sense. In a learner-centred classroom, where teaching and learning are purposeful and contextualised, decisions must be focused (hopefully at least partially directed by learners) and responsive to needs.

An alternative to a preplanned schedule for thinking is the At a Glance Thinking Guide (page 69). This is designed to assist teachers with planning to make the links between the thinking skill, teacher questions and activities. Thinking skills have been organised under three discrete headings: 'Reflection and metacognition', 'Creative thinking' and 'Logical and critical thinking'. The guide also provides example questions and comments that might be typical of students engaging in this type of thinking.

These lists are not exhaustive or intended to indicate that thinking should be discrete. Thinking can involve skills from more than one category. In addition, skills such as synthesising could be creative or critical. Compare, for example, the synthesis of statistical and qualitative data. With these considerations in mind, and to aid accessibility, the skills have been listed in one category only.

These strategies are samples only. They have been listed in only one category of thinking to avoid repetition, but many may be used in different ways and for different purposes. For example, de Bono's coloured thinking hats involve critical, creative and reflective thinking and metacognition. While it may appear that graphic organisers are not appropriate for creative thinking or thinkers who have a right-brain preference, some graphic organisers are flexible enough to be suitable for all learners. For instance, although a Venn diagram provides a particular structure, it can be started anywhere and it doesn't have a rigid sequence.

This guide is not meant to be a sequential planner. Ideally, all types of thinking would occur by the end of a sequence of learning events. The following teacher audit is designed to help teachers keep tabs on their coverage. It is not intended that activities be contrived to cover all skills in any one lesson. Again, the appropriateness of the skill and strategies is the best guide for selection. Teachers are encouraged to add to the strategies and use it as a menu of ideas to select from.

Encourage questioning and create a thinking discourse

Thinking skills should be made explicit by the teacher and become a topic of regular classroom discussion. We acknowledge the role of the teacher in promoting classroom talk about thinking, but also believe that students need to do more of the thinking and talking in classrooms. Sentence starters (see Strategy 2 on page 73) and questions initially modelled by the teacher should lead to internalisation of thinking, and the use of reflective questions should become evident in discussions.

Effective questioning is at the core of effective thinking. In general, it is useful if teachers:

- use challenging questions that require students to compare, contrast, reflect, synthesise and make judgements;
- use student questions as a basis for thinking about, hypothesising, discussing, investigating and evaluating ideas.

At a Glance Thinking Guide

I want my students to . . .			
Think . . .	So I ask . . .	So I could try . . .	Students might say . . .
Reflection and metacognition			
• Self-question • Question • Action plan • Make decisions • Apply the ideas to another situation • Recall • Summarise • Review/revise • Think about others' feelings • Think ethically	• How do you feel about . . .? • How have you changed your thinking? • As a result of what you've learnt what do you plan to do? • What would you like to find out? • Why do you think . . .? • Tell/show me what you already know about . . .	• de Bono's shoes • Debate • Question dice • Brainstorm (list, describe, name) • **Graphic organisers** • Concept map • Cluster web • Spider diagram • Bridge • Comic strip • ECG graph	• I wonder if . . . • I need to know . . . • I want to . . . • How can I . . .? • I don't know how to . . . • I think I've done a problem like this before. • Last time I did something like this I . . . • Next time I will . . . • I need to make a plan to work it out. • I remember when . . . • I know that . . . • I've learnt . . . • I feel . . .
Creative thinking			
• Create many/original ideas • Adapt ideas (add, expand, change) • Find and consider alternatives/solutions • Challenge assumptions • Imagine • Predict • Hypothesise • Plan • Invent	• Can you construct/ produce . . .? • What's the most unusual . . .? • What if . . .? • Suppose you . . .? • What would you never find/expect/see at . . .? • How many different ways could this problem be tackled? • What are some different possibilities?	• Forced relationship • Ridiculous association • BAR (bigger, add, remove) • The reverse key • Visualise • SCAMPER (substitute, combine, adapt, modify, magnify, minify, put another way, eliminate, reverse)	• What if I changed . . .? • I am not sure I agree/ believe . . . • I want to make something new. • If I added . . . • There must be other ways. • I think . . . will happen if we . . . • There's lots of ways to . . . • Why can't we try a new way?
Logical and critical thinking			
• Organise • Classify • Analyse • Examine • Critique • Generalise • Hypothesise • Synthesise • Evaluate/judge • Sequence • Rank • Prioritise • Establish cause and effect • Infer • Interpret • Consider different viewpoints • Reason	• How could you organise these ideas/objects? • What are the important factors? • If your findings are true for other . . . what can you now say about all . . .? • What would you expect might be the reason for . . .? • How could you sum up the situation? • Which would be more effective/fairest? Where do you stand? • What order do these work best in? • How would you prioritise these? • What does the data mean? • Why might this be?	• Bundling • Fat and skinny questions • Metaphors • Story map **Graphic organisers** • Cluster web • T chart • Y chart • Venn diagram • Balancing scales • Data chart • Ranking • SWOT analysis (strengths, weaknesses, opportunities and threats) • Cycle circle • Twister • Flow chart • Continuum • Consequence or futures wheel	• I can put these types together . . .. • The most important parts are . . . • I think that the . . . must . . . • When you put all the ideas together it means . . . • You need to do it in this order . . . • If you do . . . then . . . might happen. • I think that overall . . . • It could be . . . or it could mean . . . because . . . • In my opinion . . . • The author is really saying . . . • I disagree/agree because . . . • This seems to mean . . . • Not everyone would agree. . . • This should go first because . . . • When you weight up all the . . .

Some example questions are listed in the table below. (See also the Before and After Sentence Strips work sheets on pages 80 and 81).

Early in the session/unit	During the session/unit	After the session/unit
• What do you know about . . .? • What can you already do? • What do you plan to do during this session? How do you plan to do this? • What do you remember/know/ understand from the last session? • What problems/questions do you have? What can you do about this? • What do you think it would be helpful to do/think about first?	• What are you up to/doing? Why? • How will this help you? • What do you need help with? • What do you plan to do next? Why? • Do you know how to . . .? • How long will you need to do this? Why? • How can I help you? • What methods are you using? Are these effective? What other methods could you use? • What have you learnt so far?	• What have you learnt? Why? How? • What can you now do that you couldn't do before? • What do you now know that you didn't know before? • Now that you have done this today what will you need to do next time? • What/who helped you to learn? How? • What hindered your learning? Why? • What do you still need to do/learn? • Why do you think we did this?

(adapted from Wilson and Wing Jan 2003)

Plan to challenge

Students pay more attention to content and to their own thinking if the content is challenging. Much research (for example, Baird 1998) indicates that when the intellectual challenge for students is too low, we fail to engage them physically or mentally. Learning opportunities must allow for extension, creativity and critique of thinking. See Chapter 7 for examples of unit/topic ideas that promote high intellectual challenge.

Open-ended tasks, involving multiple paths and possibilities, challenge more students but, like all teaching strategies and approaches, they do not suit every learning purpose. For example, where prior knowledge needs to be determined closed questions may work best to quickly assess particular aspects of student thinking and knowledge. Other approaches are also necessary to allow teachers to access student understandings and values they may not have anticipated or planned for. When we base our teaching on where students are currently at (as opposed to where we think they should be), we have real potential to move students forward.

Involve students in assessment and goal setting

Reflection involves assessment and metacognition involves self-assessment. To promote student thinking, it is important to involve them in personal goal setting and the assessment process. Where goal setting is part of a programme, time must be allowed for regular reflection on progress towards goals. This reflection will be the context for further self-assessment and could lead to modifying goals, further assessment and so on. The following are examples of ways to include students in the assessment process:

• Ask students to identify their own thinking preferences and discuss ways to enhance thinking with the whole brain, such as a 'brain gym' where students use physical exercises to stimulate both sides of the brain (Dennison, in Ward and Daley 1993).

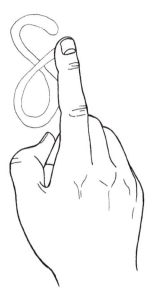

- Use student reflections on their own thinking as a basis for negotiating ways of working. For example, they may identify that they mainly use logical thinking when approaching tasks. Teachers might then ask them to use a creative thinking strategy when presenting their ideas.
- Create class charts of questions useful for self- and peer assessment purposes.
- Involve students in programme evaluation. Ask them for their critical feedback on the value of a particular lesson/unit/course. This has a different purpose to self-assessment. It involves students thinking through learning purposes and outcomes and shows students that teachers value their ideas.

See Chapter 6 for a range of other assessment ideas.

Take risks to promote respect and reflection

Where risk taking is encouraged, students are more likely to articulate their own thinking and respect others' opinions and rights. Honest, open and respectful communication requires constant attention and reflection. Students learn much from the ways teachers work with each other, talk to their students and by the examples of talk and reflection that they highlight for reflective discussions. Teachers should demonstrate the process of risk taking, to show they value a range of opinions and to reflect on the results of such discussions (see the Before and After Sentence Strips worksheets on pages 80 and 81). Encourage students to reflect aloud and explain how they are thinking and feeling about certain issues and why.

Thinking and action

Where reflective thinking causes disequilibrium, genuine action (even at the thinking level) is likely. For example, students may be reflecting on the impact of waste and the potential of recycling. Their studies may have caused them to feel uncomfortable about their own personal actions (metacognition) and they realise they could take some action to reduce waste. The content is important. If we ask students to think deeply about issues of importance to them and engage them emotionally, some sort of action that demonstrates their learning is not only useful but also likely to be initiated by them. The action itself can then also be the subject of reflection.

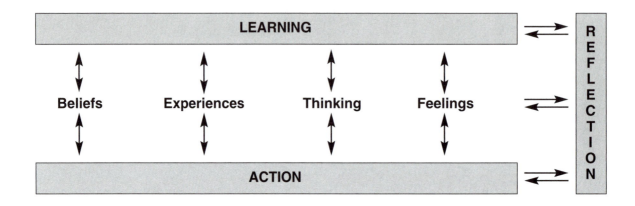

Dear Sir, I'm writing to you because the rainforests are in danger. People have been lighting fires. Not only have they been destroying the rainforest but they have all so been destroying animals of the rainforest. Is there something you can do to help stop people from doing this dreadful thing? I would appreciate if you respond to my letter soon.
        Regards,
Madison

Something to try

Strategy 1

Pulling it Apart and Putting It Back Together

This strategy can form the basis of an extended session or several sessions. It requires students to analyse, synthesise and evaluate. It is best suited to issue-based content, particularly where there are controversial and/or a range of opinions. The key words appear in bold to indicate the words that teachers could put on charts.

Directions

1. Students **explain** the issue succinctly (either orally or in written form).
2. Students **draw** the relationships if any (see the second adaptation below).
3. Students **break it up**: what are the factors involved?
4. Students identify what the different **perspectives** are.
5. Students consider how the issue could be resolved. They list the **options**.
6. Students make a **judgement** about the issue. Have them explain why they chose their option (see the third adaptation below). Their decisions can be presented to others in any way they like.

Adaptations/extensions

- Use key words as headings in individual booklets. Students use these at various times during a unit of work. Teachers could use these for assessment purposes, as higher-level thinking is involved – particularly analysis, synthesis and evaluation.

- Students show the relationships in a specific way, for example Venn diagrams; or choose from a range of options, such as cause-and-effect wheels, concept maps, mind mapping and metaphors.

- The task of making judgements could be open ended or partially directed. For example, students could choose the most ethical, sensible, suitable or feasible. Rather than all students rating with the same criteria, allocate different criteria to different groups. When discussing final judgements, the centrality of perspectives could be raised as an issue.

Strategy 2

Before and After Sentence Strips

Using the prepared sentence strips (pages 80 and 81), teachers stimulate discussion and reflection on the forthcoming unit/lesson ('before' sentence strips) or at the end of the unit/lesson ('after' sentence strips).

Directions

1. Enlarge the sentence strips onto card and cut up into separate strips. Laminate them for repeated use.
2. Place the strips into lucky dip boxes for student to select and respond to (verbally, in written or dramatic form).

Adaptations/extensions

*   Number the strips and have students pick a lucky number. Then produce the corresponding sentence strip.
*   Paste the sentence strips onto posters for student self-selection.
*   Choose a specific sentence strip for particular students.
*   Give each student a copy of the sentence strips to respond to when reflecting.
*   Copy the strips onto masking tape and place them on a die. Students roll the die and respond to the face that is showing.
*   The sentence strips could be used for individual, small group tasks or whole group reflective discussions.

Strategy 3

Independent Investigation Report

The What Have You Learnt? worksheet (page 82) assists students to structure their reflections and report on their independent investigations. It requires students to consider issues, questions and the application of their findings.

Directions

If students have not reflected on the investigation process previously, clarify the types of expectations.

Adaptations/extensions

Written prose is only one way to summarise findings. Students could be encouraged to adapt the worksheet and respond in ways they consider appropriate. For example, visual organisers, a poster or a video recording of an oral presentation could also be used. (See Chapter 6 for a list of ideas.)

Strategy 4

Look at It, Look into It and Looking Forward

This Look at It, Look into It and Looking Forward worksheet (page 83) structures thinking about an issue/problem so that students can consider different perspectives (positives, negatives, creative, personal, others and global) and requires them to consider possible actions. This is easier to complete if students have had practice using some of de Bono's thinking strategies.

Directions

1. Hand out the worksheet and discuss the sorts of responses that students might put in each box.
2. Remind students that there is no one right answer and that a range of perspectives is required. Advise students that creative thinking is required for the Looking Forward section.
3. Upon completion, make time to share these at a whole class level.

Adaptations/extensions

- Conduct this as an individual task, partially individual or completed by a team of students.
- Use the Look at It, Look into It and Looking Forward headings to structure a discussion, without requiring an individual written response for each.
- Students work in teams to collate a range of responses from each section, producing six lists of ideas. For example, students might present their lists in poster form on each of the following:
  1. What's good
  2. What's bad
  3. What's puzzling
  4. What does it mean to us (combining the responses from the 'Me' and 'My friend' boxes)
  5. A global perspective
  6. Possible actions.
- The action responses could be classified (individually, in teams or voted by the whole class) as possible, probable or preferable.

Strategy 5

Making Thinking Visual with Graphic Organisers

Graphic organisers (also called visual organisers) can be a powerful way to develop thinking skills and make students' thinking more explicit, both to themselves and others. Graphic organisers are widely used beyond the classroom. They can be a highly effective form of communication that requires few words. Teachers can adapt various organisers to suit a range of purposes, but it is important that the intended purpose is clear and the chosen organiser the most suitable for the kind of thinking involved. It is a good idea to build a classroom display showing the different kinds of organisers that are available.

Directions

1. Introduce the use of graphic organisers by showing students some examples. Create one in front of the students using a well-known topic, but one that is different from the current unit/topic. Keep a lookout for examples of visual information in newspapers, magazines, etc. and share these with your students.
2. Discuss with students what they think might be the characteristics of an effective graphic organiser. List these to assist students as they create their own.
3. Depending on the purpose of the task, select a graphic organiser and explain to students that they will use it to 'show what they are thinking', or to help them 'think something through' more clearly.
4. Give students time to draft the way they might present their ideas before creating their final product. Explain to them, however, that the purpose of the strategy is not to create a work of art, but to do some thinking. We have seen some very attractive graphic organisers with very little content.
5. It is important to question students as they create their organisers. For example, ask them to 'talk you through' their diagram and explain what it shows. Also ask how it is helping them to think or what it shows about their thinking.

Adaptations/extensions

*   Use graphic organisers at the beginning and end of a unit to help track student progress and to assist students with self-assessment.
*   Design a rubric to help students assess the quality of their work.
*   Use computer programs to explore the digital creation of graphic organisers. Software programs like Inspiration and Kidspiration are ideal for developing concept maps and mind maps.
*   Encourage students to devise their own organisers.
*   Use graphic organisers to communicate information and instructions around the classroom.

Making Thinking Visual with Graphic Organisers

KEY PURPOSE OF THE ORGANISER	SAMPLE GRAPHIC ORGANISERS		
Recalling, grouping, classifying, summarising ideas	Spider diagram	Affinity/cluster web	Concept map
Sequencing events, ordering ideas	Cycle circle	Flow chart	Twister
Showing causal links (cause and effect)	Futures wheel	Bridge	Fishbone
Deeper analysis – dissecting an idea into specific components and exploring different attributes	Y chart	T chart	Venn diagram
Planning and decision making or reviewing	Scales	Comic strip	ECG graph

SNAPSHOT

Introducing de Bono's hats to broaden student thinking during literature discussions

Sue Lalor-Capewell

Sue wanted to use de Bono's coloured thinking hats to extend student thinking and to promote more thoughtful classroom discussions of literature. Sue and others in the planning team (David from the local secondary school and Jeni from the university) initially brainstormed a list of questions associated with different coloured hat thinking to use with the novel Sue was reading to the class. She had collected real 'granny' hats in each of the colours for students to use as props (and prompts) when organising their thoughts. She noticed that previously reluctant students, particularly boys, put on the hats and voluntarily joined in and, more importantly, led the literature discussions.

She then used the de Bono's hats strategy as part of a Literature Contract for home reading. She negotiated the number of questions to be answered from each hat colour and students completed the contract at home. Some of these finished products were absolutely astounding in their presentations – green hat thinking at its best. Parents commented on the use of the hats at home.

The confidence and independence de Bono's hats strategy gave to her students in their learning resulted in a much more critical exploration of ideas related to literature, enjoyment of the texts and, unexpectedly, deeper thinking across other aspects of the curriculum.

The following are student comments made about the introduction of de Bono's hats for literature discussions:

'You learn to think in all sorts of different ways and from different points of view. When we thought of something we grabbed a hat and said it. That was fun.'

'When we first had the hats in the room I thought they were things little kids did, but then I realised anyone can do them and they're a fun way of different ways to think.'

David also successfully implemented the hats into his Year 8 programme. His students also enjoyed the novelty and were able to engage in higher levels of thinking with this tool.

Learner-centred Thinking Teacher Audit

REFLECTIVE THINKING AND METACOGNITION

Have you asked your students to:

- [ ] Recall what they know, feel, believe and have experienced?
- [ ] Summarise their learning so far?
- [ ] Plan for their learning?
- [ ] Ask questions about their own thinking, learning and the world?
- [ ] Pose questions about what they have learnt/want to learn?
- [ ] Be involved in their action planning?
- [ ] Make decisions about the learning process?
- [ ] Apply their ideas to another situation/their life?
- [ ] Make judgements about their progress?
- [ ] Review what and how they have learnt?
- [ ] Consider how their ideas have changed?
- [ ] Consider how others might feel or think about the issue?

CREATIVE THINKING

Have you asked your students to:

- [ ] Create original ideas?
- [ ] Adapt ideas by adding, expanding or changing ideas?
- [ ] Find and consider alternatives/solutions?
- [ ] Challenge assumptions?
- [ ] Imagine how things could be?
- [ ] Make predictions/hypothesise about what they might find out?

LOGICAL AND CRITICAL THINKING

Have you asked your students to:

- [ ] Organise and classify information and ideas?
- [ ] Analyse data and information?
- [ ] Examine and critique data and information?
- [ ] Generalise about ideas and findings?
- [ ] Hypothesise about ideas?
- [ ] Synthesise collected data or diverse data sets?
- [ ] Make judgements or evaluate ideas?
- [ ] Sequence ideas and plans?
- [ ] Rank and prioritise ideas?
- [ ] Deduce cause and effect relationships?
- [ ] Interpret and make inferences about data?

NB This list is a guide for teachers who wish to include a variety of thinking within their programme. The selection of thinking skills and strategies used within any program will depend on the teacher's purposes. See also the At a Glance Thinking Guide on page 69.

Before Sentence Strips

I already know . . .

I am wondering about . . .

My hypothesis is . . .

I predict . . .

This is what I think might happen

This is how I am going to find out

This is what I plan to do

My question is . . .

First I need to . . .

I will need help . . .

I feel . . .

I think we should . . .

I plan to . . .

I'm not sure about . . .

I think we're learning about this because . . .

After Sentence Strips

This is how I will evaluate my plan

This is how I will evaluate my findings

I have learnt . . .

The most important thing that I have learnt is . . .

Now I plan to . . .

This is how I plan to use my new knowledge/skills

I can now . . .

I now know . . .

I will always remember . . .

I still wonder . . .

I will evaluate my . . .

I feel . . .

This is important to me because. . .

I was surprised that . . .

I am most proud of . . .

I wish I had . . .

I need to improve . . .

The best part of this is . . .

I would have liked to . . .

I got a lot better at . . .

Personalised Learning in the Primary Classroom © Kath Murdoch and Jeni Wilson, Routledge, 2008

MY WORKSHEET
What Have You Learnt?

Name: _____

What did you do?

_____

_____

What resources were useful?

_____

_____

What were the important findings?

_____

_____

QUESTIONS YOU HAD AT THE BEGINNING	
What questions were unanswered?	What new questions did your investigation raise?

Why do you think this study was important?

_____

How will you use these findings? What will you do?

_____

What would you change if you did this again?

_____

What have you learnt about yourself as a learner?

_____

MY WORKSHEET

Look at It, Look into It and Looking Forward

Name: _____

LOOK AT IT

What's the issue/problem?

What's good?	What's bad?	What's puzzling?

LOOK INTO IT

What does it mean?

To me	My friend	Beyond

LOOKING FORWARD

What can I do about it?

Action 1	Action 2	Action 3

6   The message that matters
Linking assessment to learning

Teaching and learning principles

- Assessment strategies should lead to improved student learning.
- Assessment data should inform ongoing planning and feedback to students.
- Assessment is more authentic and powerful when it is embedded within everyday learning experiences.
- A range of assessment strategies should be planned to allow all students to demonstrate what they know and can do.
- When learners are involved in the assessment process they can assume more responsibility for their learning.
- Assessment results should provide guidance and information to various stakeholders and inform teacher decision making.
- Assessment processes should demonstrate what is valued.
- Assessment can impact on students and their learning in positive and negative ways.
- Assessment should recognise prior learning and celebrate student achievements and progress.

Introductory statement

The primary purpose of assessment is to improve student learning. When this is clearly the focus of assessment, decisions about what should and should not be assessed are easier to make. Strategic assessment is intended to inform teachers about what students need to do. Accurate and effective assessment is fundamental to making informed teacher decisions for learning.

Our assessment principles should match our learning principles. These assessment principles should be reflected in our assessment practices and demonstrate what we, as teachers, believe is important for learning. If we test spelling once a week, we convey the message that we think spelling is very important. If we never give students and parents feedback on cooperative skills, our silence indicates that this has less value.

Some important questions are: What do we believe is important? What is the purpose of assessment? What will we use the assessment data for? Does our assessment reflect what we value?

Whenever possible we encourage teachers to involve students, peers, parents, other teachers and support personnel in the assessment process. Preparation, including skilling others, may be necessary. For example, although our students can reflect on their own learning, we would not expect them to be able to do so without first modelling and explaining what we hope to achieve.

Self- and peer assessment are becoming increasingly popular because this involves higher-order thinking and has the potential to motivate learners to understand requirements and to take more responsibility for their own learning. These processes provide insights into student thinking and learning that are not possible through other means.

Traditionally, assessment has been viewed as summative, and this has often been associated with a lot of stress for students and teachers. Students perform better when they are not anxious. Therefore, by weaving assessment into everyday classroom activities, students are able to show what they know and can do more easily and accurately.

When the programme (and assessment) is varied and caters for a range of different types of learners, we may better assess student performance and progress. For example, creative alternatives to traditional types of assessment, such as a role-play, can allow kinaesthetic learners the opportunity to demonstrate their understandings.

If classroom activities represent significant, authentic teaching and learning purposes then each activity should provide valuable assessment data. When a range of assessment data is collected in an ongoing way, no student should be disadvantaged (see the Assessment Plan on page 89). Students should feel that assessment is a valuable process and a constructive record of their achievements.

Making it happen: guidelines for assessment

Plan for assessment

Planning for teaching is important and so is planning for assessment. At a theoretical level, teachers should use the teaching and learning principles above to guide their planning. At a practical level, and to minimise the work involved, starting with the classroom programme can be useful. This is based on the assumption that activities are focused and planned to develop particular knowledge, skills, values and attitudes. Our plans for learning should include assessment.

The following points are worth remembering when planning for assessment:

- **Decide** what is to be assessed.
- **Aim** for what is manageable over the week/term/unit.
- **Focus** on a group of students or aspect of learning.
- Work with peers to create **criteria** for assessment and processes for moderation if necessary.

- Select a **range** of assessment types (such as performance, visual, written).
- Keep easily **accessible records** of planned and unplanned outcomes.
- **Involve** others.
- **Use data** gathering for future planning.

Key activities for assessment can be easily identified in planning documents with a highlighter (for pen and paper documents) or by using another font (for electronic documents).

Involve students and others in assessment

The advantages of involving others in assessment (particularly students) far outweigh the potential problems sometimes raised by teachers. One way to involve students is to engage them in designing criteria, self- and peer assessment. As stated earlier, we cannot expect students to know automatically what and how to assess. Explain the purposes to students, and give them models (if possible) and explicit ongoing coaching to make self-assessment useful to them and others. Generally, students underrate their performance, so it is important to provide constructive feedback on their assessments.

In order for students to want to self-assess (this can sometimes mean exposing their weaknesses), they need to recognise that everyone has strengths and needs and that this acknowledgement is important for improvement. Teacher honesty and modelling can be helpful in the classroom. Where team building and trusting cooperative relationships have been established, self-assessment is easier. One issue facing teachers when considering self-assessment is that students must be trusted to take responsibility for their own learning. Teachers can demonstrate that some of the classroom decision making can be shared, for example classroom organisation, rules and reporting processes

The following are some suggestions for increasing students' abilities to be reflective learners, which is fundamental to self-assessment:

- Make time to discuss learning in small groups and with the whole class.
- List and model reflective questions (see Wilson and Wing Jan 2003, 1993).
- Make charts that show thinking about classroom topics, for example 'What we know' and 'What we would like to find out'.
- Develop class, group and individual goals.
- Write reflective journal entries (teacher and students).
- Display reflective sentence starters. For example: 'I feel proud that I can . . .', 'I wonder . . .', and 'I am able to . . .' (see Chapter 5).
- Involve students in programme evaluation.
- Negotiate criteria for assessment.
- Conduct peer assessment panels.
- Have students keep records of their own achievements.
- Promote positive discussion about self (student, peers and teacher).

Make goals explicit and negotiable

Just as teachers find teaching goals useful for guiding planning and evaluation, students will find that navigating their learning experiences will be easier if goals are explicit and negotiated according to individual needs. Although this can be challenging for the teacher, student goal setting and reflection is a worthwhile process that can and should be built into classroom teaching for students of all ages.

When setting goals consider:

- where students are currently at
- what is the goal
- what is achievable
- time lines
- parameters for the process
- ways of tracking progress
- involvement of students and others
- amount of possible negotiation.

Use a range of assessment types

As students learn, process and communicate their learning in a variety of ways. A range of assessment types should be used, such as written or performance (see the Assessment Plan on page 89). In fact, assessment should be a useful, and hopefully enjoyable, learning experience. No one assessment strategy or type will give all the information that is required or suit all learners.

The following is some general advice for all assessment strategies:

- Ensure that all students understand how to complete the assessment tasks and their purpose.
- If criteria are used they should be made clear to students prior to beginning the task.
- Check your interpretation of students' work is accurate by discussing it with students and moderating with other teachers.
- Use the assessment data as one piece of evidence and verify with other data (and assessment types).
- Keep assessment data to compare progress over time.

The Assessment Plan on page 89 provides some examples of different assessment types and general advantages and disadvantages for that type. Please note that while the various types are treated separately here, many strategies require multi-modal assessment tasks that traverse types and learning areas.

A note about self-assessment: Many of the strategies above could involve self-assessment. Self-assessment can be represented in more than just written form.

A note about tests: Many commercially available tests may be useful when used as diagnostic tools, but in general the best tests are those designed by the teacher or students and matching the curriculum content and purposes. It should be remembered that written tests can assess only a part of the desired curriculum and need to be verified with other assessment data. Students do not perform better under stressful situations, so to avoid anxiety tests should be used strategically and as part of the classroom activities.

Assessment Plan

Assessment types and examples	Advantages	Disadvantages
Performance-based assessment		
• Demonstrations (science, sport, etc.) • Role-play/dance/ songs • Physical freeze-frames • Experiments	• Caters for students who find it difficult to express their ideas in written or verbal English. • Can be a novel and enjoyable way to assess. • Can model to others. • Provides a context for reflection on learning. • Allows students, particularly kinaesthetic learners, an alternative to traditional assessment types.	• Some students feel this form of assessment is too public and/or find it uncomfortable. • May inhibit responses that could be expressed through other more private means. • Sometimes the point is lost amongst attempts to be funny, dramatic, etc.
Written tasks		
• Student-designed tests and quizzes • Class charts • Cloze • Reflective journals • Speeches • Poetry • Position statements/ papers • Reports • Projects/investigations • Rating scales	• A written record is provided for accountability purposes. • Written records can be filed and used for later reference, for example at parent–teacher interviews. • Written records can be compared easily for making judgements about progress.	• Can be difficult for students who do not have written English-language skills or confidence. • Privileges students who are usually doing well in a traditional verbal–linguistic style classroom.
Visual tasks		
• Constructions/models (e.g. dioramas) • Computer simulations • Paintings, drawings, diagrams, collages • Graphic organisers (e.g. data charts, concept maps, flow charts)	• Can provide a lot of information succinctly. • Caters for students who find it difficult to express their ideas in written or verbal English. • For some students, this is the clearest way to show their understandings.	• Sometimes visual records still need interpreting and accompanying written text to clarify significant points. • The products can take up a lot of space.
Oral tasks		
• Peer presentations • Retelling • Debates • Panel discussions • Student and teacher questioning • Audio/video recordings • Songs/raps	• Students may express their viewpoint better than if they were asked to write it down. • Allows for some creativity and integration of various assessment types. • Students can learn from the oral presentations of others.	• Some students feel this form of assessment is threatening (e.g. second-language learners and students with disabilities). • May limit responses that could be expressed in more detail through other means. • Oral presentations can be time consuming.
Technology (many of the above can also be represented technologically)		
• PowerPoint presentations • Spreadsheets and graphs • Inspiration • Graphic organisers	• Caters for students who are confident with this medium. • Good for students with poor handwriting and those with poor spelling and grammar, as these can be checked.	• The computer programs can be restrictive in what can be represented – careful selection is required. • Students can be sidetracked easily with various program gimmicks.

Track progress

Assessment and record keeping are pointless unless they are useful for planning future learning. Therefore, procedures need to be fair, valid, reliable and accessible. Teacher moderation of results can assist with consistency and equity issues.

Various examples of assessment have already been listed, some of which are also useful for keeping records, such as class charts and computer-generated files. Other forms of record keeping are listed below:

- **Portfolios** are a systematic collection of work and reflections over time. They have the potential to involve students and parents in the learning and record-keeping processes.
- **Checklists** focus on particular aspects of learning (can be annotated).
- **Class lists** focus on individual students.
- **Anecdotal notes** provide comments and observations on student learning.
- **Profiles** map progress over time, based on a variety of assessments.
- **Self-assessment** allows students to keep records of their own progress in various forms.

Some aspects of these records can be documented digitally.

To organise record keeping effectively:

- plan the focus of record keeping
- take notes/enter data during teaching time
- establish a routine for recording data on each child and different aspects of learning
- involve others (students, parents, specialists, etc.) in record keeping.

Something to try

Strategy 1

Peer Feedback

Providing peer feedback can be very engaging, but also a very challenging task. Although students generally enjoy it they may not wish to criticise their peers. Having an agreed set of criteria can help. Consider using a rubric or the Peer Feedback worksheet (page 97).

Directions

1. Ask students to brainstorm what they consider to be important for the particular task being peer assessed. For example, organisation, a range of well-sourced information and creativity.
2. Students may wish to use a rating scale or consider techniques for commenting on the criteria.
3. Have students set up a peer assessment table (for the panel). After each presentation the panel spends time discussing the appropriate feedback.

It is important that all assessors are well aware of the criteria and that other parameters are well understood. For example, no personal criticism is allowed, but criticism of ideas is accepted.

Adaptations/extensions

- Peer assessors complete written feedback sheets (such as the one provided on page 97) individually or as a group.
- Include self-assessment and/or teacher assessment on the peer feedback sheets that are developed.
- Students use the feedback from peers to create a self-assessment action plan for further learning.

Strategy 2

Metaphorically Speaking

As an alternative to written and oral communication assessment tasks, this strategy requires students to describe their learning through images. Students can select and draw or metaphorically describe their own learning using the Pictures of My Learning worksheet (page 98).

Directions

1. Students visualise themselves learning. Ask them which if any of the following images could represent their efforts: a snail, a sponge, a person blindfolded, etc. They could make suggestions about appropriate images.
2. Students create images of their own learning using the following cues: thinking, feelings, progress. Some students might like to offer ideas. Students who are visual learners and those with a right-brain preference will find this easiest.
3. Show them the Pictures of My Learning worksheet, which asks them to select and create images and metaphors. Check if there are any questions, as this is likely to be a new approach for many learners.
4. Allow time for students to share their images and metaphors.

Adaptations/extensions

- Students use drama to show how they feel about their learning, progress or a more specific aspect of their learning such as a cooperative skill. Freeze-frames work well for this (see Chapter 2).
- Use the worksheet as a starting point for students to think about different ways to describe their own learning. Students do not need to represent their own learning in the same way as others in the classroom.

Strategy 3

Design a Rubric

Rubrics are gaining popularity as one way to plan for assessment and record keeping, and involve students. Some teachers find it hard to be specific about assessment criteria and ways to distinguish between various levels of achievement; however, this skill develops with practice. We have worked with students who are able to design their own rubrics. The Design a Rubric worksheet (page 99) assists students to design their own criteria and rating scale. Think carefully about what is suitable for rubric ratings. The rating of dispositions, for example open mindedness, is very difficult.

Directions

1. Demonstrate the construction of a standard class rubric.
2. Using the worksheet, ask students to select learning aims to list on the rubric. Write some on the board as examples.
3. Discuss how you could rate performance. For example: 1–4 or OK–Excellent.
4. Students think of examples of different performances.
5. Students identify the level they want to work towards. If they underestimate their own performance, suggest they aim higher.

Note: If this is the students' first experience of designing a rubric, you may choose to complete no 1 on the worksheet for them, or at least make several suggestions. You might also advise students that the rubric criteria are negotiable and that they must be approved by you.

Adaptations/extensions

- Introduce the rubrics to certain groups at the same time and develop group criteria. Criteria are best done individually.
- Complete parts of the rubric (such as the aims) for students before allowing them to complete other grid cells.
- Use the rubrics for further self-assessment reflections.
- Students use the rubrics to rate their own performance. Use them yourself to make judgments about learning.
- Send a copy home to inform parents about assessment criteria.

Science Project Rubric Assessment

Topic: _____

Name: _____ Form: _____

Met Deadline?   Yes   No

	Excellent	Good	Fair	Not Satisfactory
Depth of understanding	Made all important connections between all ideas. Thorough and complete understanding.	Made some important connections between ideas. Substantial understanding.	Made a few connections between ideas. Partial and incomplete information.	Made no connections between ideas. Some misunderstandings and misconceptions.
Accuracy	All the information (facts, concepts and understandings) was accurate.	Most of the information was accurate and inaccuracies didn't affect the overall understanding.	Some of the information was accurate. The inaccuracies affected the work.	Much of the information was inaccurate. Errors affected the quality of work.
Clarity	Exceptionally clear and easy to follow.	Generally clear, easy to follow.	Lacks clarity, difficult to follow.	Unclear, disjointed information, impossible to follow.
Planning	Thorough planning – identified all information and resource needs and set goals.	Effective planning – identified most information and resource needs and set some goals.	Moderately effective planning – identified some information and resource needs and set a few goals.	Ineffective planning – didn't include information and resource needs or set goals.
Implementation	Highly effective approach to gathering and sorting information.	Effective approach to gathering and sorting information.	Moderately effective approach to gathering and sorting information.	Ineffective approach to gathering and sorting information.
Representing findings	Highly effective presentation of findings using appropriate formats.	Effective presentation of findings using some appropriate formats.	Moderately effective presentation of findings using a limited range of formats.	Presentation of findings not effective.
Work habits	Completed the work independently.	Completed the work with minimal assistance.	Completed the work with moderate assistance.	Needed considerable assistance to complete the work.

Strategy 4

Show Me What You Know

This strategy is very open ended, allowing all students to select a technique that best shows what they know or can do. This may be used to demonstrate understanding gained over a short period or a more extended sequence.

Directions

1. Advise students that you want to assess their learning and that they can do this in a range of ways.

2. It is important for students to first identify what they will show (that is, the knowledge or skill).

3. Students then select a technique that they believe will best demonstrate their learning. The Show Me What You Know and What You Can Do worksheet (page 100) provides some examples.

Adaptations/extensions

*   Limit or signal the preferred type of learning.

*   Direct different students towards or away from a particular method. Not all students need to perform the same technique.

*   Students work individually or in small groups.

Strategy 5

Learning Maps

Students' metacognition can be enhanced by reviewing explicitly both what and how they have learned. In this strategy, students use visual organisers to represent their learning over a period of time. This may be over one lesson or a whole term's work.

Directions

1. Students think back over the work they have done during a given time period. You may wish to create a list of activities/tasks they can use as a prompt for their mapping. It can be useful to have students close their eyes and visualise the work they have done or to spend time looking back through journals or learning logs to remind them of what they have done.

2. Students create a visual representation of their learning journey over the unit/ lesson. They need to include:
    *   a selection of the activities/tasks they undertook (they name these and describe them in some way)
    *   the sequence of learning tasks
    *   what they learnt from each one and how they felt about their learning
    *   an overall statement/symbol to represent their learning throughout the unit.

3. Provide students with a selection of possible graphic organisers for the mapping exercise. Some of the most relevant ones for this purpose include bridge, ECG graph, flow chart, twister and comic strip. Use the ideas on the Making Thinking Visual with Graphic Organisers worksheet (page 77).

4. Upon completion, students compare maps and analyse why they may have responded to the content in different ways.

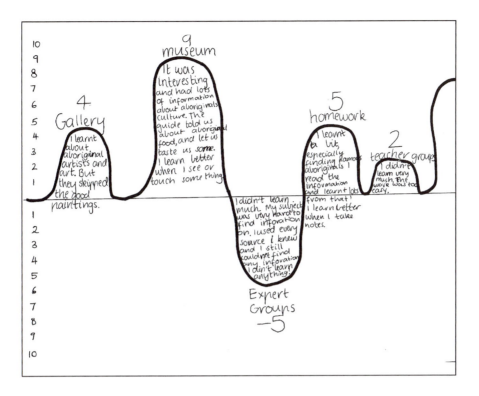

Adaptations/extensions

- Conduct this strategy as a class or in small groups. Students can create collective maps of a unit.
- Invite parents or other students to view the learning maps students have created at the end of a unit.
- Students gradually build their maps during a unit of work.

SNAPSHOT

Involving students in the assessment process

Natalie Miller and Rebecca Hoyne

Rebecca and Natalie wanted to use multiple intelligence activities as part of their integrated curriculum contracts. Student self- and peer assessment evolved from this work. A sub-committee of students designed an assessment rubric group for the project, which was used for self- and peer assessment of project achievements.

Assessment criteria for contract work

Tick or highlight the criteria once you have completed your contract.

Assessor's name: **Presenter's name:**

	Good	Very good	Excellent
Planning	List	List plus diagram	Thorough detailed plan
Contents	At least one understanding	Shows one or more understanding	Demonstrates as many understandings as possible
	Clear	Understandable; sequenced	Focussed and logical
Presentation (written)	Neat	No mistakes; decoration	Colourful and informative
Presentation (oral)	Clear voice	Loud and expressive	Things to show and questions
Presentation (creative)	Interesting design	Colourful	Detailed and creative

Peer assessment

_____

_____

_____

_____

_____

Teacher assessment

_____

_____

_____

_____

_____

In the following weeks, students worked independently on their projects. When they were ready they signed up for two tasks – one was to present their work and the other to take part in the peer assessment panel. The latter was extremely popular and taken very seriously.

Peer assessment panels were appointed for each project presentation. These were taken from the register in order. The panel members (five assessors, including at least one teacher) were seated at tables at the back of the room. Each had a copy of the student-negotiated peer assessment sheet. Their task was to record their feedback honestly and constructively on the sheet. After students had presented, each panel member had an opportunity to give their feedback orally. This was encouraging for student presenters, good for the self-esteem of panel members and reinforced the criteria to the student audience who were yet to present. The students gave excellent feedback demonstrating their understanding of the project requirements.

When the project was completed students attached their self-assessment. They also received the peer assessment sheets and comments from their teacher. In this way students received more reflection and feedback than usual.

MY WORKSHEET
Peer Feedback

Name: _____

EXAMPLE CRITERIA	OWN CRITERIA		
Preparation/organisation • Planned presentation • Logical order • • •	• • • • •		
Presentation tools • Used visual aids • Used multimedia • • •	• • • • •		
Voice • Spoke clearly • Spoke loudly • Used expression • Looked at the audience • Involved the audience • Answered questions well •	• • • • • • •		
Other criteria Overall comments			

MY WORKSHEET
Pictures of My Learning

Name: _____

Circle the picture that best describes your effort.

Draw or describe your . . .

Thinking

Feelings about learning

Progress

Sum up your learning (in words, using a metaphor or pictures)

MY WORKSHEET

Design a Rubric

Name: _____

1. **Select your aims.**
   For example: the way you work with others; how much information you include

2. **Select your own grading.**
   For example: OK, Good, Excellent

3. **Write examples of what your work would look like using your selected aims and gradings.**

GRADING →			
AIMS ↓			

MY WORKSHEET

Show Me What You Know and What You Can Do

Name: _____

People/Self

Choose to work on any of the tasks individually or with others. Reflect on your learning and participation in group tasks.

Logic and maths

Show the data using a:
- [ ] time line
- [ ] flow chart
- [ ] graph
- [ ] order of events
- [ ] recipe
- [ ]
- [ ]
- [ ]

Space and vision

- [ ] Draw/paint
- [ ] Design a poster
- [ ] Draw a cartoon
- [ ] Design symbols to represent the main ideas from the data
- [ ] Use a visual organiser (mind map, flow chart, Venn diagram, etc.)
- [ ] Create a comic strip
- [ ]

Body

- [ ] Create a series of 'body shapes'
- [ ] Devise a simple scenario/role-play
- [ ] Use your bodies to express feelings/ emotions/issues raised
- [ ] Conduct a mock interview/debate
- [ ] Video a performance
- [ ]
- [ ]
- [ ]

Music

- [ ] Innovate on a known song or tune – write new words for a familiar tune to illustrate key themes/feelings arising from the data
- [ ] Create a rap
- [ ] Make sound effects
- [ ] Create a sound story
- [ ]
- [ ]
- [ ]

Word

- [ ] Write a list/chart
- [ ] Create a fact file
- [ ] Write a report, letter, narrative
- [ ] Write a newspaper article with a headline
- [ ] Write slogans
- [ ] Prepare a spoken report
- [ ]
- [ ]
- [ ]

7 Planning with purpose
Pathways for curriculum planning

Teaching and learning principles

- Collaborative planning produces a richer and more coherent curriculum.
- Students should play an increasingly active role in planning for their learning.
- Forward planning enables teachers to keep the 'big picture' in mind.
- Curriculum planning is, in itself, a form of professional development.
- Whilst curriculum policies and guidelines provide an important reference point, it is teachers' knowledge of their students that is the most critical factor in planning decisions.
- The best planning is goal driven – activities are selected to meet goals rather than as an end in themselves.
- An inquiry framework can be a valuable planning tool for fostering lifelong learning skills and integrating the curriculum.
- An integrated approach to planning can enhance student learning and strengthen staff teams.

Introductory statement

The process of learning is often described as a journey. The plans we make as teachers are the maps that help us guide our students on their journeys. Through our planning, we clarify destinations and work out the best pathways to lead to them. Our plans enable us to create a kind of bird's-eye view of our work, to maintain a focus on the big picture and to examine the links between activities, our teaching purposes and our students' learning needs. At its best, planning can be not only a powerful tool to make our day-to-day teaching more purposeful, connected and organised, but also a process that stimulates regular reflection on, evaluation and celebration of the work we are doing.

Effective planning for today's classrooms is a highly skilled and strategic process. Not only are we responsible for mapping relevant, worthwhile pathways for our students, we must ensure that students are actively involved in setting the direction their learning will take. Skilled planners know how to make the most of the resources available to them, and they do this within the context of their students' needs and characteristics.

Teaching and learning plans go beyond merely selecting or devising activities – they must identify multiple outcomes and goals, consider appropriate strategies, meet individual needs, build in assessment, attend to grouping and other management strategies, and consider connections across learning areas. In addition, plans are often one of the means by which teachers are held 'accountable' for their work. The way in which planning is documented and evaluated is an important consideration in relation to this accountability. Although some planning is personal and relates to specific details for teaching, the majority should be an open, collective and shared process, available to all stakeholders in students' learning.

High-quality, collaborative planning takes time. For this reason, an increasing number of schools are recognising the need for extended periods of time, within the school week, to enable teachers to plan; and to plan in teams. Allocating a half- to full day per term for planning, in addition to regular meeting times, encourages the kind of 'big picture' and long-range thinking required.

Most teachers engage in ongoing, informal and incidental planning. They plan 'on their feet', make jottings in work programmes or diaries and come up with ideas in the car on the way to school! Some of the best teaching moments arise out of spontaneous events – windows of opportunity that present themselves unexpectedly in the course of a day or teaching session. However, even these opportunities are maximised when placed in the context of clear 'big picture' goals and visions. This chapter focuses on the more explicit, deliberate plans teachers make to support students' learning.

Making it happen: guidelines for planning

Do less, better

If ever there was a mantra for our times, this is it. Across the world, the teaching profession has recognised that the curriculum is overloaded. While more and more has been added to the expectations of teachers, very little seems to have been removed. This, together with the rapid explosion of knowledge and increased access to information through new technologies, means that careful decisions need to be made about what to include in and exclude from our planning. Our focus needs to turn to those things that are transferable across learning areas and into 'the real world'. We need to ask ourselves: What are the 'big ideas' in this? What generic skills will my students gain from this? How can we link the ideas in this experience/subject area to other learning experiences the students might have? How can we create connected learning experiences where several goals or outcomes might be dealt with simultaneously? Our planning must move away from the notion of covering as much as possible and towards working with ideas in all their complexity. Our aim should be for increased depth and connectedness.

Embed planning time into the school day

As planning becomes increasingly important to the development of lifelong learners, significant time must be made available for teachers within the context of the school day.

Staff can think and work creatively to free up time for sustained, collaborative planning on a regular basis. Some schools use some of their pupil-free days across the year to focus on planning. To plan for student-centred learning, teams need more than a rushed meeting while students are in specialist programmes. These time slots may work well for fine-tuning and reflection, but initial planning and mapping need a sustained block. Some schools utilise staff meeting times for team/whole school planning. Administrative work is done each fortnight rather than weekly (and more of this can now be done through the intranet), allowing alternative meetings to focus on the curriculum. We have found that the more time allocated for planning and reflecting within the school day, the more willing teachers are to 'top up' that time outside of school hours.

Develop a shared vision of what and how students will learn

Mapping the curriculum is important. We owe it to our students to have a clear vision of how their learning experiences unfold from year to year. Regardless of the subject area or grade level, planning and teaching are greatly enhanced when they are viewed within the wider framework of students' learning experiences across levels and subjects. Successful schools see this mapping process as a collaborative task. All teachers should be involved in considering the 'big questions' that underpin their curriculum. Students and parents can also play a significant role in constructing the curriculum. This involvement may be through the negotiation of the curriculum on a day-to-day basis or through more formal channels of devising scope and sequence documents. Developing a shared vision and map for student learning involves all stakeholders in considering some important questions, such as those below:

- What do we believe about learning and teaching? What are the shared visions and understandings we have? Where do our views differ? How does this impact on our work?

- What do we consider to be some of the important skills, values and qualities to develop in our students?

- What are the characteristics and needs of the students in our community? What do we need to emphasise in mapping our particular curriculum?

- What are the broad understandings about the social, physical and personal world that we think all students should be exploring during their time at our school?

- What do we currently teach? How does this align with our 'big picture' ideas? Where are the gaps?

- What links are there between subject or learning areas? How can we make more sensible connections between these areas?

- What matters to our students? What are they interested in? How can we value these things in the context of the wider picture we have for their learning?

- How can we accommodate the learning styles and preferences held by our students?

- How do our assessment and reporting processes align with our curriculum map and our teaching and learning processes?

Plan collaboratively

Effective, collaborative planning can be the key to success in designing, implementing and assessing a learner-centred curriculum. When teachers plan in teams they learn from each other and utilise individual strengths; there are built-in checks and balances to judge the worth of particular activities; reflection is stimulated through discussion; and the load can be shared. An effective planning team can also be one of the most powerful contexts for professional learning. When setting up teams for curriculum planning, time should be spent establishing clear protocols for working together and clear roles within the group. Teacher groups should reflect regularly on how well they are functioning as a group. The checklists and proformas at the end of this chapter are useful frameworks for encouraging shared planning and discussion. In addition, we have observed a range of structures that help learning teams work effectively. Examples include:

- establishing roles in the group (team leader, recorder, etc.)
- setting agendas for each meeting
- maintaining a clear emphasis on planning and reflection, rather than the more surface-level administration that can be done in written or electronic form
- bringing student work to the meeting and discussing the evidence of learning contained in the work samples
- using shared planning proformas.

Make connections between learning areas

Throughout this book, we have advocated integrated, learner-centred approaches to teaching and learning. When authentic connections are made between learning areas, students are generally more engaged and are able to develop a range of skills in context. Planning for an integrated curriculum also encourages staff to work in teams and to consider their collective responsibility in developing big picture understandings and generic learning skills. Not all aspects of students' learning should be integrated. Teachers need to make strategic decisions about the links they will make between areas. Authentic links between learning areas can be determined by the extent to which those links will help students develop deeper understandings. For example, simply counting cars during an inquiry into transport will not assist any greater understanding of transport, nor will it necessarily assist the development of mathematical skills or knowledge. While integrating the curriculum has been a common approach in primary schools, many post-primary schools are now moving in this direction. Older students are highly capable of working across disciplines and using the higher-level thinking strategies this involves. The physical and logistical constraints in secondary settings have been addressed by many teachers eager for new learning opportunities for their students.

Include students in the planning process

When students have the opportunity to make some decisions about what and how they will learn, they are more likely to engage in their learning. While we believe that teachers have an important responsibility to take students beyond their interests, we also recognise the value of asking students what is important for them to learn. When students are genuinely involved in planning aspects of the curriculum, they feel a stronger ownership of their learning, leading to greater responsibility and self-management. Planning for our own learning also teaches students some important skills in decision making, communication, problem solving, forecasting, compromising and negotiating. Throughout this book, there are several examples of strategies that involve students in planning for learning.

Year 9 students were asked to identify personal and global questions and concerns. The questions below were shared and used to inform curriculum planning.

- Will there ever be world peace?
- Will it become harder or easier to get a job?
- Will I have a family?
- Where will I live?
- Will they cure deadly diseases?
- Will the world end in my lifetime?

Focus on the big picture

It is worth restating that the content of curricula needs to be considered in new ways. Given the vast quantity of information available to students and the rapid rate of knowledge growth and change, our purpose must go beyond covering a set of prescribed outcomes. Curriculum planning needs to link content to big ideas; to transferable concepts and understandings. It needs to make connections between students' questions and new ideas. It is imperative that teachers plan with these connections in mind. For example, teachers planning to include a study of earthworms in their programme need to consider what 'big ideas' the topic will help students to understand. These concepts may include cycles, interdependence and change. By focusing on the big picture, teachers become more mindful of the connections they can make across learning areas and through different topics. The same concepts, for example, can be revisited through a study of family life, wetlands or recycling, or identified in aspects of maths, art or health. Similarly, the skills and qualities we aim to develop in our programmes can go beyond a subject or lesson-specific plan. Learning to ask effective questions, for example, can be planned for across many subject areas and contexts. Whilst the choice of topic or specific content for our planning is important, it is the big picture ideas and the generic skills behind them that will be the most robust in the long term.

Focus on inquiry

Using an integrated, inquiry-based approach to curriculum planning is an effective way to maintain a big picture focus, actively engage students and meaningfully link learning areas. Integrated inquiry emphasises the development of deep understandings and the connections across learning areas. While we recommend an integrated approach to inquiry, inquiry methodology can be applied effectively to a subject area. Common to the approach is the selection of generative topics that encourage students to investigate significant issues and questions across disciplines. We have included some basic guidelines in the remainder of this chapter (see pages 107–8).

Some frameworks for curriculum planning

The ideas in this section are presented as proformas, tables and checklists rather than strategies. They are intended to help teachers reflect on and finetune key aspects of their planning.

Pathways for inquiry

In general, planning for inquiry helps ensure a more learner-centred curriculum. Inquiry learning is based on the assumption that students bring some prior knowledge/experience to a topic and that this needs to be acknowledged and built upon. Inquiry also involves students in asking questions about issues/ideas that are relevant to them and investigating answers to those questions. It is active rather than passive; emphasising process as well as content; structured and sequenced, rather than sporadic and disconnected. While we believe inquiry is enhanced by integrating the curriculum, it can be used to plan learning within particular disciplines.

The following table outlines some possible pathways for inquiry. The pathways, or starting points, are not mutually exclusive. Aspects of one may be used in conjunction with another. Importantly, the approaches used are not presented in hierarchical or sequential form. We do not regard any approach as more desirable than others. The use of the approach will depend, as always, on the needs of the students (and the age group to some extent), the nature of the content being explored and the time available. Most students will benefit from a range of approaches.

Some pathways for inquiry

Approach	Advantages	Challenges	Examples
Negotiated Students plan a personal or small group investigation based on a topic or question of their choice (usually within a defined area). They may sign an agreed contract.	• Significant level of choice over inquiry content/topic/method. • High degree of engagement and ownership of learning. • Caters well for different learning styles, preferences, needs and interests. • Students act as models for each other. • Fosters self-directed and independent learning.	• Teachers need to ensure students are taken beyond current understandings and experiences. • This approach requires very astute observation, record keeping, time management and individual assessment skills. • Resources are needed to cover a range of topics.	Contracts: • Issues/problem based (see below) • Interest based (e.g. sports, music and animals) • Play based (see below)
Play based Students explore a range of materials within or outside the classroom. Through strategic teacher interaction, whole class, small group or individual inquiry may develop from discoveries or observations made during play.	• Particularly suitable for early learners. • Non-threatening and open ended – allowing each child to explore at their own pace and level. • Promotes decision making, independent and small group interaction. • Can involve a high level of sustained and focused dialogue between students, and between teachers and students. • Highly engaging due to the direct and hands-on nature of the play. • Students' questions, interests and experiences are used as the basis for inquiry, ensuring ownership and connectedness.	• Can be limited by the availability of stimulating materials or by teachers' uncertainty. • Teachers' questioning skills need to be of a high level. • Systematic monitoring and record keeping required. • Topics/inquiries emerging from play experiences can lack generative significance. • If not well designed, may not result in inquiries that extend children beyond the known/familiar.	Depends on the materials provided. For example: • Natural/environmental objects, living things, such as plants and animals • Construction material • Water play • Household items, old calendars, postcards, scales • Puzzles
Issue or problem based Problems or issues in the school, community or wider world are identified (by students or teachers). Students consider possible actions/solutions to address the problem or meet the goal. They design questions to guide inquiries.	• A highly authentic form of inquiry. • Links real-world situations with real purposes. • Relevance fosters a high level of engagement. • Teaching occurs at the point of need and is immediately transferred to a real-life application. • Students experience active citizenship. • Results are often publicly acknowledged, providing positive reinforcement for learning.	• Difficult to plan ahead. • Teachers need the flexibility to respond to problems/issues. • Need to check worth of investigation regarding significant ideas/concepts/skills • High level of organisation skills (for both teachers and students) required to manage the action plans. • Must rely on commitment from community members and other non-school personnel.	• School-based issues such as bullying, student leadership, uniforms, canteens, playground design and playground rubbish. • Events such as sports days and performances. • Common projects such as creating a vegetable garden, recycling systems, healthy lunch week and energy reduction. • Community issues such as the use of open space and facilities for young people.

Approach	Advantages	Challenges	Examples
	• Related tasks/activities (across learning areas) designed to assist students at the point of need.	• Teachers need to think creatively about the purposeful relationship between the project/ learning areas.	• World issues such as social and environmental projects (e.g. use of plastic bags).
Shared inquiry units The topic or question is usually determined by the teacher, but may be negotiated with the class. Sequence of phases: moving from prior knowledge to investigation, processing and drawing conclusions, reflecting and applying knowledge in some way.	• Creates a strong sense of community in the classroom. • Teachers plan ahead to ensure quality resources and experiences. • Teachers can ensure the content is challenging and relevant. • Tasks can be supported systematically by regular routines and specialist subjects.	• Shared inquiry units can lack personal engagement for all students. • Teachers need a strong repertoire of strategies/ approaches to ensure 'felt purpose' for students. • Teachers need to ensure that authentic experiences are embedded. • Students' questions must be catered for.	• Can be developed around any topic of significance. From specific topics such as the life of an earthworm, to broader topics such as 'heroes'. • Integrated curriculum topic. • Can be based on a current issue or problem.

Planning thoughtfully: an audit sheet

The grid on page 109 gives teachers a set of reminders to use when planning. While the sheet is general in nature, it will be helpful for teachers mapping out an extended, learner-centred unit of work.

What's the big idea?	Selecting resources
☐ Is the topic/focus generative in nature? Does it connect to significant concepts about the way the world works? ☐ Is this topic relevant to these students? ☐ Does it have the potential to teach skills and content from a range of learning areas? ☐ Could the topic make a difference to the students' thinking? To their actions? To the way they see and work with others? ☐ Will the topic be intellectually challenging for these students? ☐ Is the topic planned to connect students emotionally?	☐ Can this topic be resourced by real-life, authentic experiences? ☐ Can the students gather first-hand data? ☐ Are there a range of resources available from which students can access information (written, visual, human, other)? ☐ Are the resources inclusive? Do they (collectively) offer a range of viewpoints? ☐ Can the resources be used in a range of ways for different purposes?
Strategies for learning	**Assessment**
☐ Are strategies included to ascertain students' prior knowledge and experience? ☐ Are students given some choice/ownership over what and how they will learn? ☐ Is there a wide variety of strategies to meet the individual needs/learning styles of students? ☐ Do strategies require students to use several skills? ☐ Do the strategies aim for active participation by all students? ☐ Are strategies transferable? Will students be working in ways they can adapt to other learning situations? ☐ Are the strategies open ended? Do they allow students to work at a range of levels towards a range of outcomes? ☐ Are strategies/learning experiences sequenced in order to effectively scaffold students' learning over time? ☐ Are thinking skills included in the explicit planning for this topic?	☐ What understandings, attitudes, skills and values will be assessed? ☐ Has information about students' prior knowledge/skills been recorded for later reference? ☐ Is there a range of strategies used to allow all students to demonstrate what they understand and can do? ☐ Are assessment strategies embedded into the ongoing teaching programme? ☐ Are specific arrangements in place to help students assess their own learning and the learning of their peers? ☐ Are assessment criteria identified and understood by students? ☐ Have students participated in designing the criteria? Are assessment strategies linked to teachers' purposes? ☐ Are arrangements in place for teams of teachers to moderate students' work in order to assess understanding fairly?
Making a difference	**Grouping**
☐ Do students have the opportunity to act on what they have learnt? Are there avenues to act on their understanding? ☐ Have connections been made between the local and global spheres? ☐ How will the learning be celebrated and shared beyond the classroom? ☐ How will students be encouraged to reflect on what and how they have learned? ☐ How will students' personal goals be identified and met during this unit? ☐ Is the community, or individuals within it, involved in this unit?	☐ How and when will students experience collaborative learning during this unit? ☐ How will the unit allow for diverse groupings – individual, paired, interest based, friendship based, etc.? ☐ Has time for reflection on group processes been factored in to the unit? ☐ What measures are in place for individual accountability on group work?

Starting points for integrated inquiries

The following table provides a few examples of effective starting points for inquiry-based learning. The ideas include many that we have developed in our recent work with teachers in both primary and post-primary settings. The list is not intended to be prescriptive or exhaustive; rather, it will act as a stimulus for your own planning regardless of the age level you teach. The use of a key question, or set of questions, can help provide an overarching focus for an integrative unit.

Sample topics for inquiry (shared, negotiated or play based)	Sample issues/projects for inquiries
• **Moving along:** How do moving objects work? Why and how do we use moving objects? How can we make something that moves along? • **Looking after No. 1:** How can we care for our bodies? Why do people knowingly harm their bodies? • **In the garden:** What different plants and animals live in our gardens? What roles do they play? How do they interact? • **You've got a friend:** Why are friends important to us? What are the different kinds of relationships we have in our lives? How do relationships change? • **No place like home:** How and why do people seek homes in new countries? • **Going, going, gone:** Why do some animals and plants become endangered? What's our role and responsibility? • **Kids in the kitchen:** How is cooking a science? How and why do we change food when we cook with it? What happens when we combine various foods? How and why can food be preserved? • **Behind the scene:** How does popular culture affect us and how does it change over time? • **When the going gets tough:** How do people set and face challenges in their lives? Why do people seek out adventure? • **Waste not, want not:** Why is waste a problem? What can be done to manage the waste humans produce? • **Let me entertain you:** Why do humans seek entertainment? How do views of entertainment change across time and place? • **Making life easier:** How has technology changed our lives? Does it make life easier? • **Follow the leader:** What makes a good leader? How do different groups of people organise their leadership? Do we need leaders? • **Working for a living:** What is work? What are the different kinds of work available to people? Why do people need or choose to work or not work?	• How can we deal with **bullying** in our school? • What kind of **canteen** should we have? What food should be sold? • How can we design a **playground** to meet the needs of students in this school? • How can we create a **garden** that will be sustainable within a school environment? • How can we use **water/energy** in more sustainable ways? • What kind of **website/page** would best represent our school/class? • How can we **recycle** the waste in our school? • How can we create an end-of-year **performance** that will showcase our strengths? • How can we attract more native **birds/animals** to our garden? • What can we do to support **refugees/homeless/ disadvantaged** people in the UK? • How can we make a difference to **children** in developing countries? • What can we do about our endangered **animals**? • How can we help our local community meet the needs of **young people**? • How can we help prevent the influence of **drugs** on ourselves and others? • What kind of **diet** is right for us? How can we find out how to eat for good health? • How can we **communicate** our learning at school to others in the wider community? • How can we create a **classroom environment/ school playground** that is more conducive to learning? • How can we encourage the school and wider community to participate in more **physical activity**? • What kind of **uniform** do we want for our school? • What can we do about **pollution** in the local river?

A basic overview of the inquiry process

ON GOING REFLECTION	**Selection of Topic**	A **generative topic** that allows for the development of broad, overarching understandings, links learning areas, has relevance to students and lends itself to direct experience/first-hand data. May be teacher selected or negotiated with students.
	Generative Question/s	What is the unit really about? What are the key ideas? What questions will guide the inquiry?
	Understandings, Skills and Values	What do we want students to **understand** by the end of the unit? What is important to know about this? What key skills and values will be enriched through this inquiry?
	Tuning In	Engagement and gathering prior knowledge, pre-assessment, **questions for inquiry**, goal setting. Sometimes students will require some immersion in the topic if little is known/ experienced.
	Finding Out	Experiences and texts that **add to the knowledge base**. Emphasis on gathering first-hand data in a range of ways (usually shared experiences).
	Sorting Out	**Organising, analysing and communicating** the information gathered using a range of vehicles (e.g. through Maths, Art, English, Drama, Music or Design & Technology).
	Going Further	Raising **new questions**, **extending experiences**, **challenging assumptions**. May be negotiated individually.
	Drawing Conclusions	Stating understandings. What do we know now? How do we feel? High-level thinking about the topic. Identifying avenues for action and application.
	Reflecting and Acting	Now what? Taking action. Reflecting on the unit: what, how and why learning has come about. What did I learn about this topic? What did I learn about myself? What should I do now?

SNAPSHOT

Cross curriculum negotiated programme

Lidia Foskett and Wendy Richmond

Lidia and Wendy's curriculum planning is developed around the premise that children have the right to learn in a variety of ways and to make choices about their own education. To that end, their weekly programme is based on a negotiated contract system where they set a minimum requirement for what they want each student to achieve. The students are responsible for choosing when and how they complete these requirements during the week.

If students finish the teacher-specified tasks, they can pursue any project of their own choice with 'educational value'. For example, science experiments and fitness activities may be popular for a while and then other activities might be chosen.

There is minimal whole class work and expectations for each student vary. If required, the teachers plan small group workshops. Parents and other community members might also offer workshops that students can choose to attend if they wish. This means that students are usually not doing the same thing at any one time.

Bibliography

Allard, A. and Wilson, J (1995), *Gender Dimensions: Constructing Interpersonal Skills in the Classroom*, Eleanor Curtain Publishing, South Yarra.

Allard, A., Bretherton, D. and Collins, L. (1992), *Afters: Gender and Conflict in After School Care Programs*, Melbourne University Press, Vic.

Atkins, J. (1993), 'How students learn: A framework for effective teaching', IARTV Seminar series, no. 22, Melbourne.

Baird, J. (1998), 'A view of quality in teaching', in *International Handbook of Science Education,* eds Fraser, B. J. and Tobin, K., Dordrecht, Netherlands.

Beane, J. (1997), *Curriculum Integration*, Teachers College Press, San Francisco.

Coil, C. (1999), *Teacher's Toolbox: Integrating Instruction and Units*, Hawker Brownlow, Melbourne.

Darling-Hammond, L. (2000), 'Teacher quality and student achievement: A review of State policy evidence,' in *Education Policy Analysis Archives*, vol. 8, no. 1.

Dennison in Ward, C. and Daley, J. (1993), *Learning to Learn: Strategies for Accelerating Learning and Boosting Performance*, Switched On Publications, Queensland.

Gardner, H. (1983), 2nd edn 1993, *Frames of Mind: The Theory of Multiple Intelligences*, Basic Books, New York.

Guild, P. and Garger, S. (1985), *Marching to Different Drummers*, Basic Books, New York.

McGrath, H. and Noble, T. (1995), *Seven Ways at Once*, Pearson, South Australia.

Queensland Dept of Education (2001), *New Basics*, available at http://education.qld.gov.au.corporate/newbasics.

Rogers, W. (1995), *Behaviour Management: A Whole-school Approach*, Scholastic Books, Australia.

Wilson, J. and Wing Jan, L. (1993), *Thinking for Themselves*, Eleanor Curtain Publishing, South Yarra.

Wilson, J. and Wing Jan, L. (2003), *Focus on Inquiry*, Curriculum Corporation, Carlton South.

Further reading

Australian Council of Deans of Education (2001), *New Learning: A Charter for Australian Education*, Canberra.

Bennett, B. and Rolheiser, C. (2001), *Beyond Monet: The Artful Science of Instructional Integration*, Bookation Inc, Toronto, Ontario.

Blythe, T. et al. (1997), *The Teaching for Understanding Guide,* Jossey-Bass, San Fransisco.

Collis, M. and Dalton, J. (1990), *Becoming Responsible Learners: Strategies for Positive Classroom Management*, Eleanor Curtain Publishing, South Yarra.

Costa, A. (1992), *The School as a Home for the Mind*, Hawker Brownlow, Melbourne.

Department of Education, Training and Youth Affairs (2001), *PD 2000 Australia: A National Mapping of School Teacher Professional Development*, DETYA, Canberra.

Education Department of Western Australia (2001), *Success for All: Selecting Appropriate Learning Strategies*, Curriculum Corporation, Carlton South.

English, R. and Dean, S. (2001), *Show Me How to Learn: Practical Guidelines for Creating a Learning Community*, Curriculum Corporation, Carlton South.

Fehring, H. and Wilson, J. (1995), *Keying into Assessment*, Oxford, Melbourne.

Frangheim, E. (1998), *Reflections on Classroom Thinking Strategies*, Rodin Educational Publishing, Loganholme.

Hayes-Jacobs, H. (1997), *Mapping the Big Picture: Integrating Curriculum and Assessment K–12*, Association for Supervision and Curriculum Development, Alexandria, VA.

Herrmann, N. (1989), *The Creative Brain*, Brain Books, North Carolina.

Hicks, D. (1994), *Educating for the Future: A Practical Classroom Guide*, World Wide Fund for Nature, Panda House, UK.

Hill, S. and Hill, T. (1990), *The Collaborative Classroom: A Guide to Cooperative Learning*, Eleanor Curtain Publishing, South Yarra.

Hill, S. and Hill, T. (1992), *Games that Work*, Eleanor Curtain Publishing, South Yarra.

Jensen, E. (1998), *Super Teaching*, Focus Education, Flagstaff Hill, South Australia.

Johnson, D. and Johnson, R. (1994), *Learning Together and Alone: Cooperative, Competitive and Individualistic Learning*, Allyn & Bacon, Boston, MA.

McGrath, H. and Francey, S. (1991), *Friendly Kids, Friendly Classrooms: Teaching Social Skills and Confidence in the Classroom*, Longman, Cheshire.

McGrath, H. and Noble, T. (1993), *Different Kids, Same Classroom*, Longman, Melbourne.

Ministry of Education. (1989), *Learning to Learn: Investigating Effective Learning Strategies*, Melbourne.

Murdoch, K. (1998), *Classroom Connections: Strategies for Integrated Learning,* Eleanor Curtain Publishing, South Yarra.

Murdoch, K. and Hornsby, D. (1997), *Planning Curriculum Connections*, Eleanor Curtain Publishing, South Yarra.

Nelson, G. (2001), *Ways with Community Knowledge*, PEN no. 128, Primary English Teachers Association, Marrackville, NSW.

O'Brien, K. and White, D. (2001), *The Thinking Platform: Strategies to Foster Whole Brain Learning in the Cooperative Classroom*, KD Publications, Marayong, NSW.

Pohl, M. (1997), *Teaching Thinking Skills in the Primary Years*, Hawker Brownlow, Melbourne.

Pohl, M. (2000), *Learning to Think, Thinking to Learn*, Hawker Brownlow, Melbourne.

Primary English Teachers Association (2003), *Changing Landscapes: Integrated Teaching Units*, Newtown, NSW.

Reid, J. (2002), *Managing Small Group Learning*, PETA, Newtown, NSW.

Reif-Nguyen, R. (1999), *Think Global: Global Perspectives in the Lower Primary Classroom*, Curriculum Corporation, Carlton South.

Reif-Nguyen, R. (1999), *Go Global: Global Perspectives in the Lower to Middle Secondary Classroom*, Curriculum Corporation, Carlton South.

Reif-Nguyen, R. (1999), *Look Global: Global Perspectives in the Upper Primary Classroom*, Curriculum Corporation, Carlton South.

Slavin, R. (1991), *Student Team Learning: A Practical Guide to Cooperative Learning*, 3rd edn, National Education Association, Washington DC.

Tasmanian Department of Education (2002), *Essential Learnings Framework* 1, DET.

Townsend, T. and Otero, G. (1999), *The Global Classroom: Activities to Engage Students in 3rd Millenium Shools*, Hawker Brownlow, Melbourne.

Wiggins, G. and McTighe, J. (1998), *Understanding by Design*, Association for Supervision and Curriculum Development, Alexandria, VA.

Wilson, J. and Cutting, L. (2001), *Contracts for Independent Learning*, Curriculum Corporation, Carlton South.

Wilson, J. and Wing Jan, L. (1998), *Self-assessment for Students*, Eleanor Curtain Publishing, South Yarra.

Wilson, J. and Wing Jan, L. (1998), *Integrated Assessment*, Eleanor Curtain Publishing, South Yarra.

Index